Shahla's Kitchen

Shahla's Kitchen

Cooking with Fire and Ice

Recipes for Balanced Energy and Healthy Living

Shahla Niazi

BROWN BOOKS
PUBLISHING GROUP

Shahla's Kitchen
Cooking with Fire and Ice—
Recipes for Balanced Energy
and Healthy Living

Brown Books Publishing Group
16250 Knoll Trail Drive, Suite 205
Dallas, Texas 75248
www.BrownBooks.com
(972) 381-0009

A New Era in Publishing™

ISBN 978-1-61254-150-1
LCCN 2014933747

Printed in the United States
10 9 8 7 6 5 4 3 2 1

For more information or to contact the author, please go to
www.ShahlasKitchen.com

Cover photograph: Elena Cone
www.ElenaCone.com

To my family for all their support and encouragement, especially my husband and my son for being brave enough to taste any new creations I put in front of them.

To my daughter, Khotan, who was with me through all of the hard times living as a refugee. She is my inspiration and my reason for being strong.

To my sister, who believed in my dreams and never let me give up.

To my grandmother and my mother, who taught me never to give up and always to move forward.

Contents

Acknowledgments

I thank Brown Books Publishing Group and especially the dedicated staff for their patience, understanding, and kindness. Thanks to my good friend Tracey for her friendship, encouragement, and help. I also express my appreciation to the team at the Apple store in Willow Bend Mall, especially Andrew, and to photographer Elena Cone for the cover and author photos.

I was a young Iranian girl, living a perfectly ordinary life, when my mother and father divorced and sent me to live with my grandmother in Shahi, a small town in the north. She was old and very strict, and her life in the countryside was very different from what I had known with my parents. However, when you have no choice, the only way to survive is acceptance.

Perhaps because of all that I have been through, when I look back on my childhood with my grandmother, I realize I became the person that I am today thanks to her. Now I can finally remember and honor her for all her wisdom. I am grateful for everything that she taught me and for those times when I was sick and she took care of me with her natural remedies. "Listen to your body," she always said. "If you listen carefully, your body will tell you something is wrong, and you will know how to deal with it. You can help yourself instead of going to the medicine cabinet every time you don't feel well. Use nature to bring harmony and balance to your body, mind, and soul."

My grandmother was a woman of great wisdom with a brave soul. "No matter what you are going through," she taught me, "never let fear and pain overpower your spirit. Remember who you are and focus on green days instead of dark nights." I choose always to remember her on green days.

Eventually I was forced to leave Iran and become a refugee. I lived in many places, going to new cities and countries, moving more times than I can remember. In my travels, I discovered that my grandmother's healing secrets have been around for thousands of years, and people from different parts of the world still adhere to much of what she taught me.

I found this particularly true of the women I met in the refugee camps. They knew what I was talking about when I referred to the balance of energies and natural healing, so I listened, watched, and gained more knowledge from them. I learned about the traditional system of medicine of India and Sri Lanka from an Indian woman practicing Ayurveda. A dear Chinese friend taught me everything about the yin and yang of Chinese herbal medicine. Every day I learned more about herbs, vegetables, spices, and fruits and their countless uses in helping the body, from purifying the blood to strengthening the heart.

Thinking back on this and other experiences I have had traveling all over the world, I have come to realize that women share a common ground. We are the glue in the family, the nurturers, and the rocks. Whether Chinese, Indian, Russian, or Iranian, women of very different cultures adhere to similar principals of energy balancing. They may call it by different names, but they care for their families by providing a balanced energy diet that enables healing harmony in the body. This approach to healing has been around since the beginning of the human race, and the knowledge has been passed down through generations of women.

When I was a young girl, I loved to go on long walks with my grandmother through her garden. Lush and green like an oasis, the garden was full of colorful flowers, bushes of herbs, fruits, and vegetables. It was her pride and joy. Everything down to the last petal or thorn was carefully planted and tenderly nurtured. My grandmother was a highly skilled herbalist and healer. She yearned to share her knowledge with me, and by the age of eight, I craved it. I wanted to learn everything I could, and she never missed an opportunity to teach me a lesson about the energy in food.

"Shahla, pull out that brown root covered with dirt. If you scratch the surface gently, you will smell ginger." I handed it to her and watched as she scraped it with her fingernail. The tangy odor wafted through the air.

"Ginger has hot energy. Good for an upset stomach," I said.

"That's right. Do you remember how much your stomach hurt when you had too many strawberries?"

"Yes, Nana," I said.

"What did I give you that made you feel better?"

"Fresh ginger sliced in hot water with some honey."

"Ginger has hot energy. The tea I made you balanced out the cold energy of the strawberries."

Nearly every day after school, I finished my homework and headed to my grandmother's garden. I listened to everything she taught me. I watched her heal people whom modern medicine could not help such as a man with a terrible headache and a mother who complained that her baby would not nurse. Through her experiences with them, she taught me that plants could heal.

Dear reader and fellow lover of food, this healing power is why it is important to understand the universe of herbs, roots, fruits, nuts, grains, and vegetables. All have distinctive properties that hold the keys to good health. I watched my grandmother at eighty-six years old walk with the vigor of a young woman. She never seemed to age because she understood how the food we eat affects our bodies.

My grandmother possessed the knowledge known in traditional Chinese medicine as the yin and yang of foods, which identifies the foods that invigorate and those that calm. This balance is a dietary approach known under many different names throughout history. One of the keys to the practice of balancing food techniques is to learn not only what each food provides to our bodies but also which foods are considered hot and which ones cold. This is the delicately balanced scale of life I learned about from my grandmother. She taught me that food is life, and life is made of love.

Knowing which way to tip the scale—toward hot or cold—is the key to good health and longevity. So many people today talk about being tired and needing more energy. If you learn the practice of balancing the types of energy in the foods you consume, you will find that you have more energy, better health, and a feeling of contentment.

Hot energy is related to action, movement, stamina, and strong emotion. It provides the mental and physical fuel to do what we need to do. However, it can also be calming. Think of how you feel when you do vigorous exercise, which creates hot energy in your body. Once you cool down, that hot energy brings on a sense of calm. Foods that soothe and relax the body are cold energy, but like hot energy, this can result in clearer thinking and a sense of stress-free invigoration. Similarly meditation brings about relaxation, but it also re-energizes the body and mind.

Knowledge of energy balancing is especially important to women because, in addition to health benefits, the secrets of beauty and passion reside in this balance. My grandmother taught me which dishes would encourage ardor and romance, which foods would stimulate a lover's stamina and excitement, and which ones cooled down the fervor.

In the following pages, I will share these and many other secrets of my grandmother's kitchen. All the information in my book is based on my personal experience and folk medicine which has been around for thousands of years. You may want to consult your physician before using any dry or fresh herbs, oils, and ingredients. I believe a hot and cold energy balanced diet is beneficial for most people, but you and your physician should decide if it is for you.

Over the years, I have created countless recipes based on my grandmother's teachings and on my own instinct for dishes that are delicious, healthful, and pleasing to the eye. Enjoy!

Everything produces energy, from the solar system to the most apparently insignificant plant in the garden. The food we eat is no exception, and using that energy to heal and balance our bodies is the philosophy of *Shahla's Kitchen: Cooking with Fire and Ice.*

In these pages, we turn back the clock and return to a time when people understood the powerful energy in fresh fruits, vegetables, juices, and herbal teas. You will learn the secrets of cooking that result in a healthier, more vibrant, and beautiful you. This is not another guide to losing weight. Rather, it teaches a way of living that puts you in touch with your body and the energies of the universe that enable it to heal. The journey begins in your kitchen!

Understanding the role of energy in your diet and how to balance it will help alleviate symptoms of these and many more disorders of modern life:

- Chronic fatigue
- Arthritis
- Irritable bowel syndrome
- Poor digestion
- High blood pressure
- Skin and hair problems
- Headache
- Attention deficit disorder
- Anemia
- Insomnia
- Stress
- Hormonal imbalance

Foods, like all living things, respond to the natural energy of the area in which they are grown. In some regions of the world, many of the foods that are consumed are considered cooler in nature. Grapes, potatoes, and apples, for example, are typically grown in much cooler climates and provide cooler energy. The Nordic people grow their food in less sunshine, giving their diets more cold energy. Not all animals and plants that thrive in colder climates have cold energy. Even in cold climates, you will find hot-energy animals and plants. It is important to understand your needs for the energy and balance dispensed by each respective energy.

My grandmother used to tell me the people south of Iran were naturally hot blooded and full of energy and passion because they lived in an area that produces hot-energy foods. Coconuts, jalapeños, and nuts grown in the southern parts of the world are considered high energy and hot.

Some foods such as small red or purple potatoes are neutral. Their dark color associates them with hot energy. However, a potato, through the marvel of nature, balances itself with its completely edible darker skin and the lighter starch within, which is cold energy. Consequently the potato tends to be neither hot nor cold. Adding butter, which is a hot property, pushes the energy of the potato into high gear, providing more hot energy.

Understanding what you want your food to do for your body is an important part of meal planning and cooking.

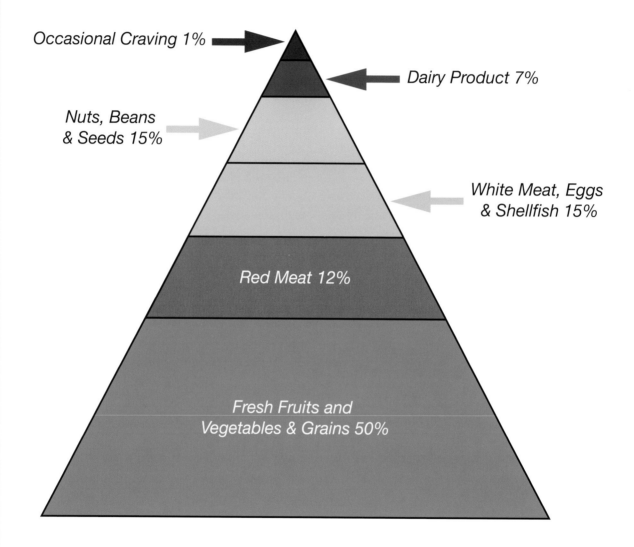

Occasional Craving 1%

Dairy Product 7%

Nuts, Beans & Seeds 15%

White Meat, Eggs & Shellfish 15%

Red Meat 12%

Fresh Fruits and Vegetables & Grains 50%

You can create your own energy-balanced diet by listening to your body and keeping this pyramid in mind. Use it as a guide for harmonizing your digestive system.

Whether you live in the north or the south, it is important to balance the cold or hot energy of the foods you eat in order to sustain the body at optimum levels of health and vitality. In these pages, I will pass on the secrets of this balancing act, showing you how to alter the property of any food from hot to cold or vice versa. For instance, pasta is a great meal in the evening because its cold energy is very relaxing. But you might not want that effect in the middle of the day, so you toss it with olive oil, which has hot properties, and the pasta dish becomes balanced.

Some foods can be too hot or too cold, or you can eat too much of one or the other. This creates what we call negative hot or negative cold energy. Think of it in terms of a runner who runs too much in one day. His body is exhausted, aching, and possibly damaged.

Although running creates positive energy, over-doing it causes problems. The same is true of foods that have negative hot or cold energy. Artificially prepared foods are a good example. Dried fruits, which seem to promote health, often contain added sugar, salt, and preservatives, all of which change the energy of the fruit to negative.

Characteristics of hot foods:
- sweet
- higher fat content
- spicy
- tend toward dry

Characteristics of cold foods:
- rich in potassium
- lower fat content
- tend toward moist

Breads, Cereals, Pasta, and Rice

White-flour products are usually neutral and don't create a balance. This includes white bread, bleached pasta, crackers, and unsweetened cereal. Even the white flour products made with sugar, like cookies and cakes, have little energy and are basically empty calories. White-flour products create negative hot and cold energy.

Whole-wheat flour products are hot energy. Be sure to note if the product is labeled "wheat" or "whole wheat." Processed-wheat flour products remove many of the vitamins, proteins, and fiber in whole wheat while whole-wheat flour products retain those nutrients.

Brown and wild rice are hot. The milling and processing of brown rice into white rice removes so many of the key vitamins that the now starch-like rice becomes very cold in nature. Even enriched rice, which is vitamin enhanced, cannot muster a tremendous amount of energy, rendering it neutral. If you prefer white rice, try to use enriched and always combine it with herbs to create balance. Otherwise, this food is best eaten in the evening.

Quinoa and hemp are hot.

Beans

Most beans are cold. However, the color of a bean can actually change its energy. For example, while most beans such as pinto, chickpeas, and lima beans are cold, kidney beans and black beans are hot.

Dairy

Most milk products are cold, with the exception of a mother's breast milk and raw goat milk. A mother's breast milk is the most natural and best source of vital energy for a newborn. The nursing mother must be careful about what she eats because she can change the energy of her breast milk, which can affect the baby's digestion. Breast milk and raw goat milk balance themselves, providing hot energy that relaxes. Most products made from milk are cold energy.

- Cheeses—cold
- Cottage cheese—cold
- Cream—cold
- Ice cream—cold
- Sour cream—cold
- Yogurt—cold

Many people drink warm milk to help them sleep because milk (even heated) has a calming effect. Often people who eat steak for dinner or another type of hot food wonder why they have so much energy before going to sleep. Balancing the meal with cold energy promotes relaxation. This is why milk has traditionally been recommended. If cinnamon, which is hot, is added to warm milk, it balances the body's blood sugar, which also creates a calming effect.

Eggs

The energy in eggs is naturally hot, but you can change the energy by preparing them in different ways. For example, sunny side-up eggs are hot, but when you flip them over and heat them to an almost hard-boiled consistency, they tend to be less hot and more neutral. Free-range chickens produce a yolk that is typically very orange. This dark-orange yolk is a great source of hot energy. The yolk of a caged chicken tends to be much paler and provides less energy.

- Hard-boiled—cold
- Soft-boiled—cold
- Poached, with a runny yolk—hot
- Raw—hot
- Omelet or scrambled—hot
- Fried—hot

Hot Meats

- All organ meats
- Beef, all cuts
- Buffalo
- Duck
- Goat
- Rabbit
- Turkey
- Venison

Cold Meats

- Bacon
- Chicken
- Lamb
- Pheasant
- Pork

Fish

All fish, including shellfish, are cold except tuna, which is hot.

Sushi is cold, although the seaweed sushi is wrapped in is hot, the white rice is cold, and the wasabi and ginger are hot. All the fish used in sushi is cold except tuna. When combined with seaweed, sushi is very well balanced. It is often served with hot sake, which has a warm energy.

Fruits

Most tropical fruits are hot except citrus fruits, which are cold. The vitamin C in citrus fruits is considered a cold energy. Commercially processed dried fruits typically contain sulfites, salt, sugar, and preservatives, making them less healthy and more on the negative-energy side.

Cold Fruits

- Apples
- Blueberries, raspberries, strawberries, gooseberries, blackberries, boysenberries
- Cherries
- Grapefruits
- Grapes (all types and colors)
- Kiwis
- Lemons
- Limes
- Oranges
- Peaches
- Pears
- Plums
- Star fruits
- Tangerines
- Watermelon

Cold Vegetables

Nearly all vegetables such as the following are cold:

- Asparagus
- Beets
- Cabbage
- Cauliflower
- Celery
- Green beans
- Green or yellow bell peppers
- Lettuce (all types)
- Peas
- Spinach
- Squash
- Tomatoes

Hot Vegetables

- Avocados
- Chili peppers
- Carrots
- Eggplant
- Jalapeños
- Mushrooms
- Potatoes—when you add butter and salt, the property of the potato changes to a negative hot energy.
  - White potatoes—cold
  - Yellow potatoes—cold
  - Red or purple potatoes—neutral

- Sweet potatoes and yams—hot
- Pumpkin
- Purple or Spanish onions
- Red bell peppers (mildly hot)
- Red cabbage

Fats and Oils

Fats and oils are hot. This includes butter as well as coconut, olive, avocado, safflower, and vegetable oils.

Herbs

Most herbs are hot, but there are some that are neutral or cold.

- Chives—hot
- Dill—hot
- Fennel—hot
- Marjoram—hot
- Mint—hot
- Oregano—hot
- Rosemary—hot
- Chamomile—neutral
- Cilantro—neutral
- Parsley—neutral
- Sage—neutral
- Basil—cold
- Lavender—cold
- Thyme—cold

Spices

Most spices are hot, except vanilla, which is neutral, and lavender, which is cold. Common table salt is processed and therefore has little, if any energy. However, sea salt, Mediterranean salt, rock salt, and other salts from natural sources have hot energy.

Seeds

Most seeds are hot. These are the exceptions:

- Sesame—neutral
- Teff—cold

Sweets

Honey, raw sugar, palm sugar, brown sugar, and other natural sugars are hot. Artificial or processed sugars are not always hot. This is because they alter the foods they are added to. For example, sugar-free Jello® is cold.

Nuts

Most nuts are hot energy, making them great snacks for a quick get-up-and-go. When they are roasted and salted, the hot energy increases.

Beverages

- Carbonated drinks (sodas) are all hot energy. If they are artificially sweetened, they become negative hot energy.
- Coffee—hot
- Sports drinks—hot
- Black, green, white, and orange pekoe teas are hot. Some herbal teas are cold. When honey or sugar is added, the energy changes.
- Beer—cold
- Champagne—very cold
- Wine (regardless of color)—cold
- Brandy—hot
- Gin—hot
- Rum—hot
- Sake—hot when heated. However, sake is made from rice, which is cold, and when it is served unheated, its energy is cold as well.
- Vodka—hot
- Whiskey—hot

About twenty years ago, while living in Australia, I met a young girl who had escaped from North China. She lived next door to me and became one of my best friends. Most afternoons, we cooked together and shared the meal with our families. Those were great times, and I learned a lot about cooking from her.

I soon discovered that our cultures had much in common. For instance, the people of North China celebrate the new year at the same time we do in Iran. There are other customs and beliefs that are very similar, but when it came to food, there were great differences. Their cuisine resembled Mongolian cooking, which is quite different. However, I was amazed to find that she balanced the energy of her dishes just like my grandmother taught me to do. When I asked her about it, she said she learned from her mother, who learned from her grandmother.

My first cooking lessons came from my Iranian grandmother. When I left my home, I traveled the world, learning from other women who shared their traditional dishes with me. The recipes that follow are my creations and recreations inspired by the vast knowledge and wisdom of these women, their mothers, and their grandmothers.

Breakfast

Cilantro and Mushroom Omelet on Toast

In Iran, the week began on Saturday, so Friday morning was like Sunday morning in a western country. Usually we had a special breakfast. The menus varied, depending on which part of the country you lived in. In the southern city of Shiraz, during winter, we would get up early in the morning and go to the bazaar to buy a lamb's head and hooves, the ingredients for *Kaleh Pacheh*. This is a traditional breakfast soup served during the cold winter months because of its hot energy. We also brought home freshly made saffron rice pudding or steamed beets and cooked carrots.

This cilantro omelet is a modern twist on simple omelets stuffed with tomatoes that we sometimes brought home on those Friday mornings. We didn't have avocado then, but now you can find avocados everywhere in Iran.

Omelets are a wonderful start to the day because of their hot energy. I also recommend them for lunch as an afternoon pick-me-up. The curry in the recipe is a hot-energy spice, but the fresh cilantro adds some balancing cold energy. This dish is high in protein as well as hot energy, so it will give you hours of vitality and balance your blood sugar.

4 servings

4 eggs

1/2 cup fresh cilantro, chopped

1/2 cup fresh parsley, chopped

1/2 teaspoon salt

1/2 teaspoon pepper

1/2 teaspoon curry powder

1/2 teaspoon paprika

2 tablespoons milk

1 cup mushrooms, cooked

2 tablespoons olive oil

2 slices whole-grain bread, toasted

1/2 avocado, mashed

1 cup fresh orange, sliced

1/2 cup strawberries, sliced

In a glass bowl, combine eggs, cilantro and parsley, salt, pepper, curry powder, paprika, milk, and mushrooms. Whisk the mixture with a fork until it is fluffy. Heat olive oil in a nonstick frying pan over medium heat. When hot, add the egg mixture and cover the pan. Cook on medium to medium low for about 5 minutes. Flip and cook for about 2 minutes more. Place the omelet on the toast and garnish with avocado. Serve with orange and strawberry slices on the side.

Cilantro and Mushroom Omelet on Toast

Healthy and Hearty Breakfast

One of my friends asked me to create a breakfast recipe that would make her family excited about waking up Saturday morning and sharing a meal together, something fun, healthy, and fast. This is for all the moms out there who, like me, are trying to encourage their families to eat healthy foods.

This dish is packed with protein and antioxidants that are sure to provide plenty of energy to start the day, and it's loaded with omega-3s for heart health. My family loves this for Sunday-morning breakfast. Avocado complements the eggs, making this hot-energy meal even hotter.

2 servings

1 beef sausage

1 teaspoon olive oil

1 egg

salt and pepper, to taste

1 whole-grain bun or bagel, split

4 slices fresh tomato

4 slices avocado

1/2 cup fresh spinach, chopped

fresh fruit

Place the whole sausage in a small pot of boiling water, which helps to leach excess salt, preservatives, fat, and artificial flavors from the meat. After boiling for 4 to 5 minutes, rinse with cold water and slice into diagonal slices. Fry in olive oil just long enough to reheat.

Fry the egg sunny-side up, being careful not to overcook the yolk. You want it to be a bit runny. Sprinkle salt and pepper on the egg.

Toast the bagel. Put the tomato slices and the fried egg on one half. On the other half, stack the avocado slices, fresh spinach, and sausage. Put the half with the avocado atop the half with the egg and enjoy! Serve with fresh fruit on the side.

Healthy and Hearty Breakfast

With plentiful hot energy to help start the day off right, this wonderful breakfast is our secret weapon before a golf tournament. The combination of ingredients creates the perfect balance of hot energy, revving up the metabolism and helping my entire family get our best scores! Anyone want to join us for a round of golf?

4 servings

6 eggs

2 tablespoons unbleached flour

salt and pepper, to taste

1/2 teaspoon paprika

1 red bell pepper, sliced thin

4 beef sausages, sliced into thin rounds

1/2 cup mozzarella cheese, shredded

2 tablespoons grapeseed oil

2 fresh tomatoes, sliced thin

1 large avocado, sliced

1 cup fresh basil, chopped

Mix eggs, flour, salt, pepper, and paprika in a bowl.

Sauté the red bell pepper and sausage rounds in a small pan with a bit of grapeseed oil for 2 minutes, then let them cool. Add the sausage and pepper to the egg mixture along with the mozzarella.

Heat grapeseed oil in a medium-sized nonstick frying pan and add the egg mixture. Cook on the stovetop over low heat, or if the pan is ovenproof, in a preheated 370° oven for 40 minutes. If you cook it on the stovetop, flip it over when it puffs up. It should take about 10 minutes to cook on each side. Just before the end of the cooking time, arrange the tomato slices on top. Garnish with avocado and fresh basil.

Spinach and Avocado Omelet

Salads

Detoxifying Salad

M y Chinese friend's grandmother created this salad recipe, which is ideal during a detox. I simply made a few changes to add nutritional value. You have probably experienced a pronounced lack of energy before doing a detox. This salad offers the hot energy you need to keep you wide awake while cucumber and zucchini, which contain plenty of water, provide essential hydration. Flaxseeds add fiber, and quinoa makes this salad hearty enough to keep you from feeling hungry soon after you eat.

4 servings

1 cup zucchini, julienned

1 cup cucumber, julienned

1 red bell pepper, julienned

1 avocado, sliced thin

1 hot chili pepper, seeds removed, sliced thin

1 cup carrots, julienned

1 cup green onion, chopped

1 cup quinoa, cooked

1 cup chickpeas, cooked

4 tablespoons olive oil

1 tablespoon sesame seed oil

2 tablespoons red wine vinegar

1 tablespoon fresh lemon juice

1 tablespoon honey

salt and pepper, to taste

1 tablespoon flaxseed

Place the zucchini, cucumber, red bell pepper, avocado, red chili pepper, carrot, green onion, quinoa, and chickpeas in a bowl and mix. In another bowl, mix the oils, red wine vinegar, lemon juice, honey, salt, pepper, and flaxseed. Pour over the salad. Toss and serve.

When I lived in Adelaide, which is located in one of the hot parts of Australia, I often made this delightful salad, which I served with pita bread. As a student with little money, I had to use my imagination to create healthy, delicious meals at little cost.

This antioxidant-packed fruit salad recipe allows you to blend the right combination of fruits to provide the best balance of hot and cold energy. If you need to feel more relaxed, increase the cold energy by adding more strawberries or grapes. For more zip, increase the hot energy by adding more of the tropical fruits such as pineapple and papaya. This recipe gives traditional fruit salad a spicy, salty kick that keeps everyone coming back for more.

2 servings

1 teaspoon honey

1 teaspoon Dijon mustard

salt and pepper, to taste

2 tablespoons olive oil

2 tablespoons fresh lime juice

1 cup fresh strawberries, sliced

1 cup fresh pineapple, chopped

1 cup grapes, purple or green, sliced

1 cup fresh papaya, chopped into small pieces

1 cup fresh melon, cut into small pieces

1 cup fresh cilantro, chopped

1 tablespoon fresh rosemary, chopped

1 tablespoon fresh mint, chopped

pita bread

In a small mixing bowl, blend the honey, Dijon mustard, salt, pepper, olive oil, and lime juice. Add the fruit and herbs to a large bowl and mix. Pour the sauce over them and mix well. Serve with pita bread.

Mediterranean Salad

Many years ago, when I was in school and working as well as taking care of my daughter by myself, I had little time to cook. Like every other mom, I felt guilty about not doing enough for my child. I worried that she was not getting enough healthy food. As a result, I developed some simple, fast, and nutritious recipes.

This dish, made with traditional Middle Eastern ingredients, is low in fat and packed full of protein to keep you and your family going on even the busiest days. The lentils, feta cheese, and chickpeas (also known as garbanzo beans) add crunch. The chickpeas contribute protein and antioxidants that help fight disease and lower cholesterol. Because of the beans and the cheese, this is primarily a cold-energy dish, but I serve it with mushrooms to balance it with hot energy.

4 servings

1 cup cherry tomatoes

1 cup mushrooms, sliced

1 cup bean sprouts

1 cup lentils, cooked

1 cup carrots, grated

1 cup spinach, chopped

1/2 cup feta cheese

1 cup mixed chickpeas and green beans

1/2 cup black olives

1/2 cup olive oil

4 tablespoons balsamic vinegar

1/2 tablespoon fresh lime juice

salt and pepper, to taste

1 tablespoon honey

Place the cherry tomatoes, mushrooms, bean sprouts, lentils, carrot, spinach, feta cheese, chickpeas and green beans, and olives in a large bowl. Toss well with your hands. In a small bowl, combine the olive oil, vinegar, lime juice, salt, pepper, and honey. Stir until well blended. Pour the sauce over the salad and toss.

The darker the mushroom, the more hot energy it carries.

This energy-boosting salad is kind to your digestive system. It's full of fiber, calcium, antioxidants, vitamin C, copper, magnesium, potassium, and vitamin K. Serve it as an appetizer before lunch or for the salad course.

2 servings

4 large figs, sliced thin

4 strawberries, sliced thin

2 kiwis, sliced into rounds

1 tablespoon organic honey

1 teaspoon lemon juice

1 tablespoon olive oil

pinch of salt

1/2 cup dry-roasted almonds, sliced

fresh mint, chopped

Arrange figs, strawberries, and kiwis on a large serving plate. Blend honey, lemon juice, olive oil, and salt. Drizzle over the fruit, and garnish with almonds and fresh mint.

Kiwi and Fig Salad

Grilled Zucchini Salad

Serve this as a salad or a light main course.

2 servings

2 medium zucchini, sliced into rounds

1 carrot, peeled and julienned

1 cup of broccoli, cut into small pieces

1/2 cup fresh rosemary and cilantro, chopped

3 tablespoons olive oil

1 tablespoon red wine vinegar

salt and pepper, to taste

1 tablespoon almonds, slivered

1 teaspoon flaxseed

Heat 1 tablespoon of the olive oil in a frying pan. Fry zucchini, carrot, and broccoli separately, no more than 3–5 minutes each, or they will be overdone. Place all the cooked vegetables on a large serving platter.

Blend herbs, remaining olive oil, vinegar, salt, and pepper and pour over the vegetables. Use your hands to mix. Sprinkle almonds and flaxseed on top.

My grandmother was a big believer in the healing power of beets. She often served them in the winter to help ward off colds and flu. Beets are also attributed with wound- and liver-healing properties. My grandmother washed my hair with beet juice to make it healthy and shiny.

Beets have lots of sodium, magnesium, calcium, iron, and folic acid. Their high fiber content helps defend the body against colon cancer and heart disease. Some cultures believe they can purify the blood as well.

This salad packs all the power of the beet and is totally nonfat. I usually drink the delicious leftover juice. By the way, don't worry if you notice that your urine turns bright red after eating this salad. That is a natural effect and not harmful.

4 servings

6 cups water

4 small beets, scrubbed

1 tablespoon honey

almonds, sliced, for garnish

Bring the water to a boil. Add the beets and boil for 30 to 45 minutes. Check with a fork for doneness—the fork should easily penetrate the beets. Let them cool in the pot for at least 30 minutes. Set on a serving plate, drizzle the honey on top, and garnish with almonds.

Beet Salad with Almonds and Honey

Soybean and Quinoa Salad

Nature has the power to heal, purify, and balance not only our bodies but also our minds and souls. I created this recipe especially for women who are going through hormonal changes such as menopause, PMS, and other hormonal imbalances.

This salad has so many benefits for your overall health that you'll want to eat it every day. It's high in fiber and packed with protein, providing the amino acids that your body needs. The high amount of calcium from the soybeans contributes to bone health, increasing the bone density in women and, as a result, conceivably protecting against osteoporosis. It supports cardiovascular health, helps alleviate menopause symptoms, and improves the digestive system. In fact, eating this salad may assist in the prevention of colon cancer. Enjoy this tasty, wonderful salad with the knowledge that it can heal you and balance your energy in mind, body, and soul.

2 servings

1 cup dry soybeans, rinsed and soaked in what is initially hot water overnight

4 cups water

1/2 cup quinoa, rinsed in cold water

2 cups water

1 zucchini, cut into small chunks

1 cup fresh cilantro, chopped

1 medium red bell pepper, cut into small chunks

salt and pepper

2 tablespoons fresh lime or lemon juice

1 tablespoon avocado oil

1 teaspoon honey

1 tablespoon red wine vinegar

Drain and rinse the soaked soybeans. Bring the 4 cups of water to a boil and add the soybeans. Boil for 5 minutes, then cook over medium heat until soft. Drain, rinse, and place in a large bowl. Bring 2 cups water to boil in the same pot and add the quinoa. Cook for 10 minutes, rinse, and add to the soybeans.

In a frying pan, cook the zucchini for 5 minutes, until it is just turning soft. Do not add salt or oil because the zucchini contains enough moisture of its own. Add the zucchini, cilantro, and red bell pepper to the soybeans and quinoa mixture. Mix the salt, pepper, avocado oil, lime or lemon juice, honey, and vinegar in a small bowl and blend. Pour the sauce over the mixture in the large bowl. Toss with two spoons and serve.

Soybean and Quinoa Salad

Rice Noodle Salad

This calming salad is best eaten in the evening. The amino acids in the hemp are very important for heart health. Carrots have lots of vitamin A, and rice noodles contribute fiber, iron, potassium, protein, and vitamins. Soybean sprouts, which balance the hormones, contain vitamins A and C, phosphorous, and amino acids. They do wonders for the skin and memory. With all these benefits, this is a salad with loads of healing power.

2 servings

6 cups water

6-ounce packet of rice noodles

pinch of salt

1 teaspoon cooking oil

2 carrots, peeled and julienned

1 cup soybean sprouts

1/2 cup snow peas, julienned

1 cup baby spinach, chopped

1/2 cup raw hemp seeds, shelled

1/2 cup quinoa, cooked (rinse and boil in 2 cups water for about 5 minutes, then drain, rinse again, and cool)

2 tablespoons avocado oil

1 tablespoon fresh lime or lemon juice

1 tablespoon red wine vinegar

1 tablespoon soy sauce

1 teaspoon honey

salt and pepper, to taste

Bring 6 cups of water to a boil. Add the rice noodles, salt, and cooking oil. Turn off the heat and cover the pan. Let the noodles sit for about 3 to 5 minutes. Transfer the noodles to a colander to drain and rinse with cold water. Gently separate with a fork and set them aside to dry.

Combine all the other ingredients in large bowl. Place the rice noodles on a cutting board and cut them into bite-size pieces. Add them to the bowl and use your hands or a fork to mix. Add salt and pepper just before serving.

Experiment with grapeseed, avocado, peanut, or roasted garlic oils for cooking. They're all high in antioxidants and vitamins D, E, and K.

Rice Noodle Salad

Side Dishes and Light Fare

Barberry Rice

Rice is one of the most popular dishes in Middle Eastern countries, and it's prepared in a variety of delicious ways. Iranian rice is mixed with saffron, slivered almonds, and orange peels. Fried dates and meats, almonds, and lots of aromatic fresh and dried herbs are added to Afghani rice. Indian rice is made with curry and all those wonderful spices. And then there are all those variations of Asian fried rice. If I close my eyes, I can still smell and taste my aunt's special rice, and now I recreate that memory in my own kitchen.

This traditional rice dish is hot or cold energy, depending on which type of rice you use. Long-grain brown rice is hot while white rice (which is highly processed) is cold. You can add balance with the type of seasoning you use. The recipe calls for basmati rice, which is hot. The lime juice and barberries are cold energy, and the almonds, saffron, and cardamom create just the right amount of hot energy.

4 servings

8 cups water

1 teaspoon salt

2 teaspoons olive oil

3 cups basmati rice

1 teaspoon saffron powder

1/2 teaspoon brown sugar

2 teaspoons hot water

1/4 cup olive oil

1 cup dried barberries

1 teaspoon honey

1 cup almonds, slivered

1 teaspoon lime juice

1 teaspoon cardamom, ground

1 large carrot, julienned

2 tablespoons plain Greek yogurt

Bring the water, salt, and 1 teaspoon of the olive oil to a boil in a large pot. Add the rice. Use a wooden spoon to stir the rice gently every few minutes, checking it for doneness every now and then. When the rice has a soft crunchy feel, drain. To the same pot, add the second teaspoon of olive oil and return the rice to the pot. Set the stove on low heat and finish cooking the rice. The same principle applies when using an electric rice cooker: Just a few minutes before the rice is fully cooked, remove the lid and add a teaspoon of olive oil. Put the lid back on and finish cooking.

Mix the saffron powder and brown sugar with the hot water in a small bowl or cup until dissolved. Add 4 big spoonfuls of the cooked rice to the saffron water, mix it well, and set aside.

In a frying pan, heat up the olive oil and cook the barberries for 2 to 3 minutes. While the barberries are cooking, add the honey. Set aside.

Cook the slivered almonds and the lime juice in the same frying pan for 2 to 3 minutes. Remove the barberry, almond, and lime juice mixture from the frying pan and set aside.

Heat a tablespoon of olive oil in the frying pan and sauté the carrots with a dash of cardomom. Set aside.

Spread the saffron rice over the remaining cooked rice. Top with the carrots. Arrange the barberries and slivered almonds around it on a large platter or a wide-rimmed bowl. Serve with Greek yogurt on the side.

Find dried barberries at Iranian and some Indian markets and specialty food stores like Whole Foods.

Saffron, prized for its intense flavor and beautiful color, is one of the most expensive spices in the world. I use ground saffron or powder, not the threads. Then spread that mixture over the rest of the rice before serving.

Barberry Rice

Green Peas and Rosemary Rice

I have a good friend who recently became a vegetarian. She asked me to teach her a few easy-to-make recipes that have lots of nutritional value. This rice recipe is ideal with chicken or fish. Its balanced cold energy is enhanced by the rosemary, which has a calming effect. Protein-packed soy contains zinc, fiber, potassium, and minerals and is beneficial for female hormonal balance.

4 servings

3 cups basmati rice

7 cups cold water

pinch of salt

3 tablespoons olive oil

1 cup soybeans, cooked

1 cup green peas, cooked

1 tablespoon fresh rosemary, chopped

1/2 cup fresh cilantro, chopped

salt and pepper, to taste

Rinse the rice with cold water. Pour into the rice cooker and add the water, a pinch of salt, and the olive oil. If you don't have a rice cooker, place a medium-size cooking pot on medium heat, and bring the water and rice to a boil, stirring every few minutes with a wooden spoon. When all the water evaporates, lower the heat and let the rice continue to cook 15–20 minutes. Taste to see if you need more salt. Combine the cooked rice with the soybeans, peas, rosemary, cilantro, salt, and pepper.

E njoy this simple and unusual dish on its own, or serve it with roasted chicken.

4 servings

1/2 teaspoon saffron powder, dissolved in 2 tablespoons water

4 cups warm water

2 cups basmati or brown rice, rinsed with cold water

pinch of salt

1 teaspoon olive oil, for rice

1 medium onion, chopped into small chunks

3 tablespoons avocado or olive oil

1/2 teaspoon turmeric

salt and pepper, to taste

1 cup dried sour cherries, rinsed with cold water

1 cup soybean sprouts

Dissolve the saffron powder in the water.

Place the water and rice in a rice cooker or pan and add the salt and olive oil.

While the rice is cooking, sauté the chopped onions in 1 tablespoon of the oil, and add turmeric, salt, and pepper. When the onions are lightly browned, add the cherries and saffron water. Simmer for about 2 to 3 minutes on low heat. Set aside.

Combine the cooked rice and sour cherry mixture in a bowl. Gently mix and serve on a platter with fresh soybean sprouts on the side.

Funky Mashed Potatoes

My son loves this dish so much that I asked him to name it. Part of what he loves is the vibrant color. The red or purple skins of the potatoes add not only to the appearance but to the healthful antioxidants in the dish. Once they are cooked and combined with the spices and herbs, the white and red potatoes change from cold energy to neutral. You can still add hot or cold energy to this dish by adding ingredients such as nuts (hot) or turkey (cold).

2 servings

6 medium red or purple potatoes, unpeeled

1/2 cup fresh parsley, chopped

1 teaspoon paprika

1 teaspoon salt

1 teaspoon pepper

juice of 1/2 fresh lime

1 tablespoon Greek yogurt

1 teaspoon butter

1 cup fresh strawberries, sliced thin

strawberries and parsley, for garnish

Bring a large pot of water to a boil. Add diced potatoes and cook until tender, approximately 20–25 minutes. Drain and transfer the potatoes to a large mixing bowl. While they are still hot, add the parsley, paprika, salt, pepper, lime juice, yogurt, and butter. Then mash. Add the strawberries to the mashed potatoes and stir. Add more salt if necessary, garnish with strawberries and fresh parsley, and serve.

wanted to create a low-fat dish the entire family would enjoy—something healthy from Mama's kitchen! This great hot-energy dish made with natural sugar, no salt, and no preservatives is packed with vitamins A, C, D, and E as well as potassium, magnesium, and more. It's low in calories if you are watching your weight, and it may be helpful in balancing your blood sugar. Most importantly, it's loaded with hot energy.

2 servings

1 small butternut squash

1 large sweet potato or yam

salt and pepper

1 tablespoon honey

1 teaspoon olive oil

1 teaspoon cinnamon, ground

Preheat the oven to 385°.

Wash the squash and slice it into thick slices. Wash the sweet potato and slice into thick slices about the same size as the squash. Place the squash and potato slices in a large glass bowl and mix. To a small bowl add the salt, pepper, honey, olive oil, and cinnamon and blend. Pour the blend over the squash-potato mixture in the large bowl. Mix with your hands and spread on a baking sheet, making sure none of the slices overlap. Roast for 45 to 50 minutes. Cool and serve.

The safest and easiest way to cut up a squash is to use a sharp knife, cut the squash in half, and scoop out the seeds and fibers. Cut each half into a quarter, and then cut each quarter into desired thickness and peel.

Sweet Potato and Butternut Squash

In this recipe, I add even more healing power to yogurt in the form of fresh herbs like cilantro, dill, parsley, rosemary, and mint, which promote healthy digestion and contain antioxidants and antibacterials that assist the immune system. Fresh rosemary helps the body fight against breast cancer, and vitamin E assists in balancing estrogen levels in women. Dill has antifungal benefits and is full of antioxidants. Mint reduces bloating and cramping and also has antioxidant powers. Choose as many or as few as you wish for this delicious and healthful treat.

2 servings

Spoon 16 ounces of plain yogurt into a bowl. Stir in 2 cups of chopped fresh herbs. Serve as a snack with flatbread or unsalted crackers or as a side dish.

My first memory of eating yogurt goes way back to when I was six or seven years old. I had a severe stomach ache caused by a virus. My grandmother made me eat steamed rice with a small bowl of yogurt for three days. I ate nothing else, and in that short time, I made a full recovery. Years later, I learned about the many wonderful things this simple food does for our bodies.

Although yogurt comes from milk, people with lactose intolerance can benefit from it. In many poor countries, when people cannot afford meat, they eat yogurt to get their animal protein and many other nutrients such as calcium, vitamins B_2 and B_{12}, potassium, magnesium, and many more vitamins and minerals.

Yogurt is useful in alleviating a great many health issues, including insomnia, stomach ulcers, diarrhea, and constipation. It can boost your immune system and your energy to keep you going throughout the day. Its calcium content helps maintain healthy bones and prevent osteoporosis, and it may reduce blood pressure. Maintaining a healthy weight is easier if you include yogurt in your diet because it makes you feel full for a longer time. Yogurt will fight against those nasty bad bacteria in your body and replace them with beneficial ones. This characteristic, along with all the good enzymes in yogurt, balances your digestive system. Your colon can benefit from it too, which means it may help protect you from colon cancer.

That's not all the good news about yogurt. It has a calming effect on children if they eat plain yogurt at night before going to bed or once or twice a day with their food. Yogurt is also a beauty food, doing wonders for your skin and hair. You might consider making a face mask with yogurt and honey. It's simple, inexpensive, and effective.

Adding fresh herbs and the right spices to cold-energy yogurt creates more flavor and adds even more nutrients to this magical food I call the "white healer." During a hot summer day, eating some yogurt will cool you down, and in winter, if you add cinnamon, fresh mint, honey, and ground caraway, it will warm you up from the inside. Everyone, from age one to ninety, can benefit from this powerful food. Make it a daily habit for yourself and your family.

Yogurt and Fresh Herbs

Yogurt and Fresh Herbs

When I lived in Australia, we spent hot summer Sundays at the beach. We always barbecued, and my contribution was this cool-energy cucumber salad, which was very popular among all my friends.

Cool Cucumber Appetizer

2 servings

2 hard-boiled eggs, mashed

1 cup canned wild or pink salmon—boneless, skinless, and drained

1/2 cup fresh cilantro, parsley, and dill, chopped

3 tablespoons olive oil

2 tablespoons fresh lemon or lime juice

salt and pepper, to taste

1/2 teaspoon cayenne pepper

1 large Lebanese cucumber, peeled or not, sliced into rounds

1/2 cup green olives, cut in half

1/2 cup blueberries

Combine eggs, salmon, chopped herbs, oil, lemon or lime juice, salt, pepper, and cayenne pepper in a bowl. Use your hands or a fork to mix everything together. Taste and adjust salt and lemon juice as needed. Set aside.

Arrange the cucumber slices on a large plate. Heap 1 tablespoon of the egg-and-salmon mixture on top of each slice and garnish with an olive half and 1 blueberry on top.

Vegetarian
Main Dishes

When I was growing up in Iran, it was a very difficult era, politically speaking. It was a time of war and revolution, and naturally, when the country is in the midst of all that turbulence, innocent people pay the highest price. We stood in a queue for hours just to buy one kilogram of meat or chicken, and it was not good-quality meat. Many people began preparing meals without meat, using mushrooms, soy such as tofu, or legumes. My family was no exception. When I moved to Australia, things were tough financially for a while. I became creative and discovered plenty of ways to make delicious and healthy meals without using any kind of meat.

Basic White Rice Recipe

I recommend basmati or long-grain Indian rice (also known as old crop). New-crop Indian rice would be sticky if you used these proportions. For the traditional stovetop method, use 3 cups water to 1 cup rice. Bring the water to a boil. Add 1/2 teaspoon salt, a little bit of olive oil, and the rice. Cover and cook until tender, approximately 10–15 minutes. If you use a rice cooker, the proportion is 2 cups water to 1 cup rice. Combine the water, rice, 1/2 teaspoon salt, and a little bit of olive oil in the cooker. It can take anywhere from 25 to 40 minutes for the rice to cook perfectly. The timer on the cooker will let you know when it's done.

Saffron Rice with Vegetarian Cutlet

This vegetarian cutlet is packed with nutrition, perfectly balanced, and satisfying even though it has no meat. If you are able, I urge you to visit an ethnic store to purchase your saffron—and I caution you that it will be a bit pricey. Much of what is sold today as saffron contains artificial flavors, especially if it is in a powder form. Saffron is treasured worldwide. In fact, in Iran and some parts of India, it is traditionally given as a gift at weddings. I still have a precious tin of saffron my aunt gave my husband and me at our wedding. Because pure saffron is potent, just a pinch will create rich flavor.

2 servings

3 cups water

2 cups brown basmati or white rice

1/2 teaspoon saffron

3 tablespoons olive oil

1 medium white potato, peeled

1 large sweet potato, peeled

1 1/2 teaspoon salt

1 teaspoon pepper

1 cup instant oatmeal

1 tablespoon fresh rosemary, cilantro, and parsley, chopped

1 teaspoon turmeric powder

2 eggs

fresh rosemary

fresh cilantro

fresh parsley

Bring the water to a boil. Add 2 cups of rice, 1 teaspoon of salt, and 2 tablespoons of olive oil. Stir and cover the pot over medium heat. Once water evaporates, add 1/2 teaspoon of saffron powder, and mix with a fork. Return cover to pot and let simmer on low heat for 15–20 minutes. Turn off the heat, cover, and set to the side.

Meanwhile boil the white and sweet potatoes. When they are tender, transfer them to a large bowl and mash. Add 1/2 teaspoon salt, 1 teaspoon pepper, oatmeal, fresh herbs, turmeric, and eggs. Combine the mixture with your hands until you reach a smooth consistency. Make round patties and fry, using the rest of the oil, for about 4 minutes on each side. Serve with rice and additional fresh herbs.

High-Protein Vegetarian Meal

When I was a child walking home from school on a snowy day in the middle of winter, I looked forward to the bowl of hot *adasy* (Persian for lentils) my grandmother always had ready for me. Oh my God, if I close my eyes, I can still smell and taste them.

This dish, full of balanced hot energy due to the red wine vinegar, mint, and fennel seed, is common throughout South Asia because it is very affordable and easy to make.

2 servings

3 tablespoons olive oil

1 cup onion, chopped

1 clove garlic, chopped

1/2 pound lentils, rinsed

3 cups vegetable broth

salt and pepper

1/2 teaspoon turmeric

1 tablespoon fennel seed

1 tablespoon red wine vinegar

1 tablespoon fresh avocado, mashed

fresh mint and rosemary, for garnish

In a medium-size cooking pot, sauté the onion and garlic in 2 tablespoons of the olive oil. After a minute or so, add the lentils and stir for about 2 minutes. Add the vegetable broth, salt, pepper, turmeric, and fennel seed. Cover and cook over medium heat for 30 minutes. Cooking times may vary depending on the age of the lentils. If necessary, add more broth and cook a little longer. Stir with a wooden spoon every 10 minutes to prevent burning. Drizzle vinegar and remaining olive oil and toss. Serve with avocado and herbs.

This is a great meal for lunch or a busy evening.

4 servings

2 cups brown rice, rinsed with cold water

5 cups water

1 teaspoon salt

1 tablespoon olive oil

1 teaspoon turmeric

1/2 teaspoon curry

3 tablespoons grapeseed oil

1 large red onion, sliced thin

2 cloves garlic, crushed

2 cups shiitake mushrooms, sliced

salt and pepper, to taste

1 teaspoon cumin seed

1 teaspoon caraway, ground

1 15-ounce can chickpeas, drained and rinsed

1 cup fresh tomato, chopped or cherry tomatoes, halved

1 tablespoon fresh rosemary, chopped

half a lemon or lime

Combine water, rice, salt, olive oil, turmeric, and curry in a medium-size pot or a rice cooker and cook until rice is soft and fluffy, approximately 35–40 minutes.

Meanwhile heat grapeseed oil in a frying pan and sauté onion, garlic, and mushrooms. Add cumin seed and ground caraway. When the onions become caramelized, add chickpeas, tomatoes, and salt and pepper. Mix all the ingredients together with a wooden spoon. Add fresh rosemary before serving over rice. If you like, squeeze half a fresh lime or lemon over the finished dish.

Mushrooms, Chickpeas, and Rice with Fresh Tomato

Cumin-Saffron Rice with Sweet Potato and Mushrooms

This vegetarian meal provides the right balance of hot energy from the grilled garlic and the sweet potato and cool energy from the rice and olives. It harmonizes the digestive system, and the endorphins in the saffron help to put you in a good mood and get a good night's sleep.

2 servings

2 cups basmati rice

1/2 teaspoon turmeric

3 tablespoons olive oil

1 large onion, sliced

2 cloves garlic

1 red potato, cut into ice-cube-size chunks

1 large sweet potato, cut into chunks

1 cup mushrooms, quartered

1/2 teaspoon saffron

1 teaspoon cumin seeds

1/2 teaspoon cardamom, ground

1 tablespoon fresh rosemary, chopped

1/2 cup black and green olives

Cook the rice with turmeric (see basic rice recipe on page 30.) Set aside.

In a frying pan, heat 2 tablespoons olive oil and add onion, garlic, red potato, and sweet potato. Cook until the potatoes are tender. Toward the end of the cooking time, add the mushrooms.

In another pot, heat 1 tablespoon olive oil and add the cooked rice. Stir in the saffron, cumin seeds, and cardamom. Cook long enough to reheat the rice and allow the spices to blend.

Sprinkle fresh rosemary on the rice and serve alongside the potatoes, with olives and roasted garlic on the side.

Roasted garlic is a tasty accompaniment to many dishes. Rub an unpeeled garlic bulb with olive oil. Wrap it in aluminum foil and place it in a preheated 370-degree oven for 20 to 30 minutes. Check it from time to time to make sure it doesn't burn. When the garlic is almost done, remove it from the oven and separate the cloves. Cook them for 2 minutes on the stovetop in a frying pan with a bit more olive oil, salt, and pepper.

Red potatoes are loaded with hot energy. I like to use them in this dish and any time I want to balance the energies by adding more heat.

Cumin-Saffron Rice with Sweet Potato and Mushrooms

Vegetarian Pasta

This recipe is the perfect balance of hot and cold energy in a simple vegetarian dish. Like most of the recipes in this book and in my other cookbook, *Healing Salads*, I created it to be simple, filling, and nutritious. The pasta in this dish possesses cold energy, but the garlic and sweet potatoes add the balance of hot energy. Sweet potatoes are also very high in vitamins B_6, B_2, and C and are a good source of manganese, copper, biotin, and fiber. If you want lovely hair and nails, you'll love this dish because biotin is great for those. Serve this at lunchtime or when you have a busy evening planned.

2 servings

10 cups water

15-ounce package organic green spinach pasta

1 onion, sliced

3 cloves garlic, crushed

1 sweet potato, peeled and sliced

1 potato, peeled and sliced

4 tablespoons olive oil

1 cup mushrooms, sliced

salt and pepper, to taste

turmeric or curry powder, to taste

1 cup snow peas

tomato wedges

1/3 cup fresh mint

1/3 cup fresh thyme

1/3 cup fresh rosemary

juice of 1 lime

1 tomato, cut into bite-size wedges

Put water in a large pot and bring to a boil. Add the green spinach pasta and cook until tender, about 10–15 minutes. Drain.

Meanwhile heat 2 tablespoons of the olive oil in a frying pan. Add the onion, garlic, sweet potato, and potato. Before the potatoes are tender, add the mushrooms, salt, pepper, and turmeric or curry powder.

Add the pasta to the potato mixture along with the snow peas and the remaining 2 tablespoons olive oil. Stir and cook for an additional 3 to 4 minutes.

Just before serving, add tomato wedges, fresh herbs, and lime juice for garnish.

Red onions are a healthy choice because of their antioxidant and anti-inflammatory powers. They also contain more iodine and phosphorous than other onions.

Vegetarian Pasta

Meat
Main Dishes

Buffalo Steak with Mushrooms and Spinach Mashed Potatoes

I traveled to northeastern Iran with my family when I was a little girl. We were invited to a relative's home for lunch. They served a steak more tender than any I had ever had and tiny mushrooms that were out of this world. After our meal, we had the customary Persian black tea with baklava. My grandmother asked what type of meat we had eaten, and she was told it was wild pig! My grandmother gave me a strange look when I asked her about it later. She said she had no idea what kind of animal had been served. Years later, I discovered that the meat of the wild pig creates lots of hot energy. Living in that cold climate, my relatives needed to eat red meats like wild pig to stay warm and healthy. When we moved to Texas, I tasted buffalo meat for the first time, and it reminded me of that wonderful steak I had long ago. I've tried to create the same dish here. Since it has hot energy, serve it for lunch or dinner before a busy evening.

4 servings

1 pound lean buffalo steak, sliced in two lengthwise for half the thickness

1 teaspoon turmeric

1 teaspoon mixed spices (cumin seeds, fennel seeds, caraway seeds, clove, curry seeds, turmeric powder, and dry lemon powder), to your taste

2 tablespoons olive oil

1 tablespoon or more soy sauce, to your taste

1 tablespoon honey

5 cups water

4 large red or purple potatoes, unpeeled

olive oil, as needed

1 cup fresh spinach, chopped

1 teaspoon paprika

salt and pepper, to taste

1 large red onion, sliced thin

2 cloves garlic, crushed and chopped

1 cup shiitake or brown mushrooms, sliced, halved, or quartered, depending on their size

1 tablespoon soy sauce

1 fresh lime

Cut the buffalo steak into long strips and place in a large bowl with turmeric, the spice mix, olive oil, soy sauce, and honey. Mix well and set aside.

Boil the potatoes in the water in a large pot. Drain and mash them with their skins, adding a bit of olive oil, until you reach your desired consistency. Stir in the spinach, paprika, salt, and pepper. Cover and set aside.

In a frying pan, cook the onion and garlic until golden brown. Stir in the mushrooms, salt, pepper, and soy sauce.

While you are cooking the mushrooms, brush a grill plate or frying pan with oil. When the pan is hot, add the buffalo strips. Turn them frequently as they will cook very quickly, in 3 to 5 minutes.

Serve the steak atop the mashed potatoes with the mushrooms on the side. Squeeze the lime over the meat and mushrooms.

Always taste as you cook, checking for salt, pepper, the right levels of spiciness and sweetness, and the correct texture to make sure you didn't overcook.

Buffalo Steak with Mushrooms and Spinach Mashed Potatoes

Strawberry-Apple Beef Roll with Asparagus

As a student in Melbourne, Australia, I worked on a beautiful apple farm owned by an elderly Italian woman. She served us various types of meat rolls for lunch and always added her fresh apples to the filling. The apple makes the meat juicier and more flavorful. They were so tasty I decided to do the same. For Mother's Day on the farm, I made meatballs for the owner. She was so happy, she cried. No one had ever cooked for her, especially on Mother's Day. Every now and then, I cook this special dish for my own mother on Mother's Day, and she loves it.

This dish has a wonderful blend of flavors, and its hot energy is balanced with cool energy. It also packs an extra punch of protein, not only from the beef but also from the asparagus, which are very high in protein. One additional plus: Asparagus is high in folic acid, which is very important for pregnant women.

4 servings

1 large onion, sliced thin

2 cloves garlic, crushed

2 tablespoons olive oil

1 pound lean beef, ground

salt and pepper, to taste

1/2 teaspoon turmeric

1 tablespoon fresh oregano

1 tablespoon fresh rosemary, chopped

1 fresh apple, grated with skin

2 tablespoons olive oil

1/2 cup strawberries, thinly sliced

1 pound fresh asparagus

fresh tarragon, cilantro, and parsley, chopped

1 fresh orange, for garnish

Brown onion and crushed garlic in olive oil.

In a mixing bowl, combine the meat, salt and pepper, turmeric, oregano, and rosemary. Mix well.

Lightly oil a cutting board or other clean flat surface. Put a little oil or water on your hands so they don't become sticky. Spread the meat mixture out like pizza dough until it is about one-fourth inch thick. Sprinkle onions and garlic, grated apple, and sliced strawberries evenly on the flattened beef. Carefully, starting at one end, roll the beef up. Heat the olive oil in a frying pan over medium heat. Transfer the beef roll to the pan, cover, and cook for 5 minutes. Flip and cook for another 5 minutes or longer if you like your beef well done.

A few minutes before the beef roll is done, trim the asparagus bottoms and cook the asparagus in the juices with the meat roll.

Slice the meat roll and serve with the asparagus. If you'd like, garnish with chopped fresh herbs and orange.

**Whenever possible, use fresh herbs for their
health benefits and wonderful aromas.**

Strawberry-Apple Beef Roll with Asparagus

Petooshi

would like to dedicate this dish to my son because we created it together and he chose the name. "What do you call a sushi-looking thing without any fish and rice, and instead you use potato and beef on top? Petooshi, of course!" he said. How could I argue with that?

This colorful dish has lots of hot energy as well as potassium, fiber, vitamin C, protein, and iron. It's perfect for lunch—simple, fast, and kid friendly.

2 servings

5 cups water

5 medium red potatoes, unpeeled

1 medium onion, sliced

4 tablespoons olive oil

1 cup broccoli, steamed

salt and pepper, to taste

1 teaspoon curry powder

1/2 teaspoon turmeric

1 tablespoon lime juice

1/2 pound rib-eye beef or similar cut, trimmed of fat

Add water to a medium-size pan and bring to boil. Add the potatoes. Meanwhile sauté the onion in 2 tablespoons olive oil until golden brown. Add broccoli once onions are sautéed. Cook about 2 minutes. When the potatoes are tender, drain and mash. Add salt and pepper. Stir the onions into the mashed potatoes, saving some for garnish. Set aside.

In a small bowl, combine the curry powder, turmeric, and lime juice.

Cut the steak into long strips about 3/4-inch wide. Use your hands to coat the steak in the combined salt, pepper, turmeric, curry powder, and lime juice. Brush 2 tablespoons olive oil on a frying pan or grill plate and heat. When it's very hot, cook the steak pieces for about 2 minutes, not more, because they overcook very easily.

It's fun for kids to help with the construction—with their hands have them form the mashed potatoes into egg shapes. Place a piece of steak on top and garnish with onions and broccoli.

Rice mixed with chopped fresh dill and served with fried fish is a traditional Iranian dish usually reserved for special occasions. In some parts of the country, this meal is served with smoked fish instead of fresh. I changed the recipe to make this beautiful rice work with any kind of meat.

This satisfying dish is healthy, colorful, delicious, and a perfect blend of hot and cold energy. The beef is hot while the herbs are cold. The rice is either hot or cold, depending on which kind you use. If you use white rice, the dish will be primarily cold. In the event brown rice is available, that would be recommended. All other rice is hot energy. The herbs are added right before serving because their flavors diminish the longer they are cooked. Green rice is a favorite of mine. I grew up eating it frequently, especially at our Now Roz (New Year) celebrations.

4 servings

1 tablespoon soy sauce

juice of 1/2 lime

1 teaspoon honey

5 tablespoons olive oil

salt and pepper, to taste

1 pound boneless beef steak, cut into thin strips

1 cup rice, preferably basmati

1 cup fresh dill, chopped

1/3 cup fresh thyme, chopped

1/3 cup fresh rosemary, chopped

1/3 cup fresh mint, chopped

1 cup fresh parsley, chopped

lettuce leaves, for garnish

1 tomato, sliced

Mix the soy sauce, lime juice, honey, 4 tablespoons olive oil, salt, and pepper to create a marinade. Add the beef strips to the marinade. Marinade at least one hour. In a frying pan or on a grill plate with 1 tablespoon olive oil, cook the beef strips for 4 to 5 minutes and set aside.

Meanwhile cook the rice (see basic rice recipe on page 30.) Five minutes before serving, add the chopped herbs to the rice and mix well. The rice will turn a lovely shade of green. Serve the meat on a lettuce leaf with the rice and a few tomato slices on the side.

Masterpiece Steak

Here's a little secret: If you're hoping for a passionate evening, be sure to serve foods with hot energy. When I was a young girl, women often came to my grandmother for advice. To protect my innocence, she would take them aside and talk to them quietly. When I got older, I realized these women were asking her what to do to get their husbands to be a little more (or a little less) passionate. My grandmother advised them, "for an evening filled with love, don't feed him fish or chicken for dinner." As an eavesdropping little girl, I was in the dark, but her wisdom became clear to me as an adult: Hot energy = passion! She had other advice for those women who were looking for a little relief. I laugh now as I remember the times my grandmother said, "Give him yogurt!"

I created this dish as a delicious, filling, hot-energy dinner.

2 servings

1 lean 8-ounce steak

salt and pepper, to taste

1 tablespoon honey

3 tablespoons grapeseed oil

1 teaspoon turmeric

1 teaspoon assorted spices, to your preference

rosemary leaves

2 tablespoons grapeseed oil or 2 tablespoons butter

3 red potatoes, cut into small pieces

1 large red onion, sliced

1 clove garlic, sliced

1 pound snow peas

5 cups water

1/2 cup fresh thyme and rosemary, for garnish

Rinse the meat, pat it dry, and set it on a large plate. Rub salt, pepper, honey, 1 tablespoon of the grapeseed oil, turmeric, assorted spices, and a few rosemary leaves into the steak. Cover in plastic wrap and refrigerate for a few hours, if you have the time. When you are ready to cook the steak, set the grill on high heat and brush the grill with 1 tablespoon grapeseed oil or butter. Grill 5 minutes on each side.

While the steak is marinating, drizzle the remaining grapeseed oil or butter over the potatoes. Either sauté the potatoes, adding the sliced onion and garlic once they've begun to cook, or roast them with the onion and garlic in a 400° oven for about 20 minutes.

Cook snow peas for 2 to 3 minutes in boiling water. Drain and rinse them with cold water to stop the cooking.

Transfer the potatoes and snow peas to a large platter. Slice the steak into 2 centimeter wide and 6 centimeter long strips and arrange on top. Garnish with fresh thyme and rosemary.

Masterpiece Steak

Meatballs and Mashed Potatoes

When I was living in Australia, I met a woman from Syria who was raising five kids by herself and working a full-time job. As so many of my friendships have, ours began in the kitchen. We shared recipes and stories about having to leave our homes. To my surprise, she had also grown up living with her grandmother. I began to notice that she served her kids different kinds of meatballs—from vegetarian to traditional—with mashed potatoes on the side. I never dared to ask her why she always gave them mashed potatoes and meatballs until, one day, she told me. "My kids are so lucky to have food on the table every night," she said. "At least they can have homemade food and a roof over their heads and be safe. When I was growing up, we had nothing to eat. Every night I use to go to bed and cry myself to sleep because I was so hungry." After that, I understood she was doing everything in her power to protect those kids. She was doing her best.

This lunch looks very heavy and filling, but it is surprisingly light and energizing. The shiitake mushrooms, red meat, and dried herbs and spices are sources of tremendous energy that last throughout the afternoon. The red onions provide vitamin C, zinc, and iodine. Zucchini, which is from the cucumber family, contains lots of moisture and essential minerals such as magnesium, calcium, and potassium.

4 servings

5 medium red potatoes

7 cups water

1 tablespoon olive oil

salt and pepper, to taste

1 pound lean beef, minced

1/2 teaspoon turmeric

1/2 cup fresh rosemary and parsley, chopped

1/2 cup oats

1 clove garlic, sliced or crushed

1 tablespoon grapeseed oil

1 red onion, sliced thin

1/2 pound mushrooms, sliced thin

2 small zucchini, sliced into rounds or small chunks

2 tablespoons tomato paste

2 cups hot water

1 bunch chard, chopped into small pieces

Place potatoes and water in medium-size pan and bring to a boil. Boil the potatoes until tender; drain and mash with the skin. While mashing, add olive oil, salt, and pepper.

Combine the meat, salt, pepper, turmeric, fresh herbs, oats, and garlic. Mix well and form into small meatballs.

In a medium pot, heat the grapeseed oil and add the onion, mushroom, and zucchini. Sauté for about 5 minutes, then stir in the tomato paste. Add hot water and mix well. Simmer for another 5 to 10 minutes. Gently drop in the meatballs one at a time. Cook for 30 to 45 minutes or until the meat is done.

Just before the meatballs are ready, sauté the chard in the oil with salt and pepper for 1 to 2 minutes. Transfer to a plate and top with the mashed potatoes and meatballs.

Meatballs and Mashed Potatoes

Buffalo Kebabs

Kebabs are a popular dish in most East Asian countries. Each region has its own variations and spices. In our neighborhood in Shahi, if people wanted to eat traditional lamb or chicken kebabs, most of them went to a restaurant, but not us. My grandmother was as accomplished as any restaurant chef and knew how to make everything. I make my kebabs exactly the way she did, but I'm using a different meat.

This light and energizing meal, best for lunch on an active day, is balanced, but it leans toward the hot side because of the red meat. Buffalo meat, which is very lean, is high in iron, making it a great meal for those who need energy. Cilantro is revered for its healing properties in many cultures. It is a soothing herb for the digestive system. Grapeseed oil has a tremendous amount of hot energy in addition to being one of the healthiest cooking oils.

4 servings

1 pound buffalo, ground

1/2 cup fresh cilantro, chopped

1 egg

1/2 apple, grated

2 tablespoons oats

1/2 teaspoon salt

1/2 teaspoon pepper

1 teaspoon lime juice

1 tablespoon grapeseed oil

flatbread

1 tomato, sliced

1/2 cup fresh parsley, chopped

sweet pickles

In a large mixing bowl, combine all of the ingredients except the flatbread, tomato, oil, parsley, and pickles. Mix with your hands and form medium-size kebabs. In a frying pan, heat the oil and fry the kebabs for 5 minutes on each side over medium heat. Serve on flatbread with sliced tomato, parsley, and if you like, sweet pickles.

The inspiration for creating this recipe came from an Afghani friend I met a long time ago. These kebabs are really little meatballs, but they are cooked just like traditional kebabs. This tasty and beautiful low-fat dish is one of the most popular in our household.

The lamb, turmeric, garlic, and herbs provide plenty of hot energy. Combining them with the cooling energy in the tomatoes, lime juice, and basmati rice creates a natural balance. There's healing power in the garlic and turmeric, which have antioxidant and anti-inflammatory properties. If you can't find lamb at your grocer's, it's worth going to a specialty butcher shop. However, if you prefer, you may use other meats, which could change the energy of this meal.

4 servings

1 pound lamb, ground

1 tablespoon rosemary

1 cup fresh parsley, chopped

1 clove of garlic, minced

1/2 teaspoon turmeric

1/2 tablespoon lime juice

1/2 teaspoon salt

1/2 teaspoon pepper

3 tablespoons olive oil

wooden skewers

1 cup cherry tomatoes

1 cup basmati rice

parsley and alfalfa sprouts, for garnish

1 large tomato, sliced

1 small onion, sliced thin

Combine the lamb, rosemary, parsley, garlic, turmeric, lime juice, salt, pepper, and olive oil. Mix with your hands and form into small kebabs. Place 3 kebabs on a skewer, alternating with 3 cherry tomatoes. Heat the grill plate to high and cook on each side for 3 to 4 minutes.

Serve with basmati rice mixed with fresh chopped parsley and alfalfa sprouts (see basic rice recipe on page 30). Lay the kebabs on top and garnish with more sprouts, tomato slices, and onion on the side.

Lamb Kebabs with Basmati

Beef Kebabs with Greek Yogurt and Fresh Herbs

Travel to any country in the Middle East or East Asia and you will encounter outdoor bazaars where anything and everything is available. I guarantee you will be drawn to the enticing aromas of the food section, where vendors make all sorts of wonderful foods. When we were little, my sister and I would take our five-dollar monthly allowance and spend it all at the bazaar on our favorite—the shish kebabs. Now I recreate them at home for my family.

The yogurt and herbs offer balancing cool energy to the hot energy of the beef in this version of kebabs. Served in a lightly grilled pita pocket, this is a delicious and refreshing meal with plenty of energy to get you through the afternoon. Plus, the calcium in the yogurt is good for your bones. Toss in a few olives to complete this sensational taste experience from my childhood.

4 servings

1 pound beef, ground

1 teaspoon salt

1 teaspoon pepper

1 teaspoon turmeric

1 onion, diced

2 cloves garlic, crushed

1/2 cup fresh parsley, chopped

1/2 cup fresh cilantro, chopped

1/2 cup fresh rosemary, chopped

1/2 cup fresh mint, chopped

2 cups Greek yogurt

1 lime, halved

salt and pepper, to taste

2 pieces pita bread, halved

Combine the meat, salt, pepper, turmeric, onion, garlic, and 1/4 cup each of parsley, cilantro, rosemary, and mint. Mix with your hands until thoroughly combined and make medium-size kebabs. Set aside.

In another bowl, mix the remaining herbs with the Greek yogurt, a dash of lime juice, and a little bit of salt and pepper.

Skewer the kebabs before or after you cook them, whichever you prefer. Heat the grill plate and grill the kebabs 3 to 4 minutes on each side. Toast the pita bread. Serve the meat on top of the herb yogurt and pitas. Drizzle some lime juice on top and garnish with cilantro.

Beef Kebabs with Greek Yogurt and Fresh Herbs

Beef and Vegetable Stew

The dried lemon and cinnamon lend a beautiful aroma to this healthy and tasty dish. Its natural hot energy is excellent comfort food for the whole family.

4 servings

4 cups basmati rice, cooked (see basic rice recipe page 30)

1 cup yellow split peas

1 large red onion, chopped

2 cloves garlic, crushed

1 teaspoon ginger, ground

1/2 pound beef, cut into small pieces

1/2 teaspoon turmeric

1/2 teaspoon cinnamon, ground

1 cup tomato paste

2 dried lemons, cut in half

1 raw sweet potato, chopped in one inch chunks

2 small red potatoes, sliced thin

4 tablespoons olive oil

salt and pepper, to taste

Boil yellow split peas in 3 cups of water until almost soft. Drain, rinse in cold water, and set aside.

Sauté onion, garlic, ginger, and beef. After a few minutes, add turmeric and cinnamon. When the meat begins to release its juices and the onion turns golden brown, add tomato paste and cook for 3 to 4 more minutes. Pour in 5 cups of boiling water and dried lemon. Cover and cook over medium heat for about 45 minutes or until the meat is tender. Add yellow split peas and the sweet potato.

Fry the potatoes in olive oil and serve them as garnish on the side, or to avoid additional fat, add them to the stew along with the sweet potato. Serve with basmati rice or pita bread.

Many Middle Eastern dishes call for dried lemon, which can be purchased in Indian and Persian markets all over the US.

Meat Main Dishes

For my son's birthday party a few years ago, I wanted to do something other than the usual pizza, something entertaining that the kids could help me make in the kitchen. They had lots of fun, but my kitchen was a mess. I know they liked our concoction because they all came back for seconds. When I asked them what we should call this dish, they named it Tooty Fruity Steak. With lots of hot energy from the red meat and well-balanced cold energy fruits, this is a quick, tasty meal, ideal for lunch.

2 servings

1/2 teaspoon turmeric

1 teaspoon honey

1 tablespoon lemon
or lime juice

1/2 teaspoon curry

3 tablespoons
grapeseed oil

salt and pepper,
to taste

1/2 pound of beef
steak strips

1/2 apple, sliced thin

1/2 pear, sliced
lengthwise

1/2 cup dried
boysenberries

1 cup mushrooms,
sliced thin

1 medium onion,
chopped

1 red bell pepper,
chopped

Combine turmeric, honey, lime juice, curry, grapeseed oil, salt, and pepper in a bowl and mix with a fork. Add steak strips and coat with the mixture using your hands or a wooden spoon.

Add the fruits and stir gently. Cover with foil and refrigerate for 1 hour, or let it sit at room temperature for 20 minutes. Heat the grill plate or frying pan and cook everything together for about 5 minutes. Serve while it's hot.

**You will find dried boysenberries at Middle
Eastern or specialty foods stores.**

Three Chubby Bell Peppers

This is a very popular dish throughout South Asia and in parts of the Mediterranean. I just made a few changes to balance the hot and cold energy.

3 servings

1 cup couscous

salt and pepper, to taste

4 tablespoons olive oil

1 tablespoon fresh lime or lemon juice

1 large onion, chopped fine

2 cloves garlic, crushed

1/2 pound beef, ground

1/2 teaspoon turmeric

1/2 teaspoon cumin seeds

1 tablespoon tomato paste

1 cup mixed herbs such as basil, mint, parsley, cilantro, oregano, chopped

1/2 cup dried gooseberries

3 large round bell peppers, any color

1 tomato, chopped fine

Preheat the oven to 375°.

Pour 2 cups of boiling water into a bowl and add the couscous, a pinch of salt, pepper, 1 tablespoon of the olive oil, and the lime or lemon juice. Mix with a fork, cover, and set aside for 20 minutes.

Heat 2 tablespoons of the olive oil in a frying pan and add the onion and garlic. Cook for 2 minutes and add the beef. Stir with a wooden spoon as it cooks and add salt, pepper, turmeric, cumin seeds, and tomato paste. Cook for at least 10 minutes. Transfer to a large mixing bowl and add couscous. Mix well with a fork. Taste and add more salt and pepper if necessary. Add herbs and gooseberries.

Carefully carve the tops out of the peppers. (You will use them later.) Scoop out the seeds and membrane. Brush inside and out with remaining olive oil. Fill the peppers with your hand or a spoon, being careful not to break them. Place the tops back on the peppers and roast them in the oven for 30 to 45 minutes. Add chopped tomato on top for garnish.

As I traveled through South Asia, I discovered that the Iranian diet is very similar to the South Asian diet, though some of the spices used and the preparation and cooking methods differ. My stay in Fiji inspired this dish.

4 to 6 servings

4 cups basmati rice

1 onion, minced

2 cloves garlic, minced

6 tablespoons olive oil

1/2 pound meat, ground (beef, chicken, or buffalo)

1 teaspoon turmeric

1 teaspoon caraway seeds

1 teaspoon cumin seeds

1 tablespoon tomato paste

salt and pepper, to taste

2 cups green beans, chopped

2 cups Greek yogurt

1 cup fresh cilantro, mint, and basil, chopped

Rinse rice with cold water and set aside.

In a medium-size frying pan, fry the onion and garlic in 2 tablespoons of the olive oil. After 2 or 3 minutes, add the meat, turmeric, caraway seeds, cumin seeds, and tomato paste. Cook for 10 minutes. Add 1 cup of warm water and simmer for 10 minutes. Set aside.

Bring 10 cups of water to a boil with salt and 2 tablespoons oil. Add rice and stir gently. Boil for 5 to 8 minutes, until it is not quite cooked. Drain and set aside. Pour 2 tablespoons of the olive oil into a rice cooker. Add 2 cups of the partially cooked rice and layer 1 cup of the meat mixture on top. Alternate layers until all the rice and meat are used. Let it cook for a while, and when you see steam when you lift the lid, use your hand or a fork to gently mix the rice and meat mixture. Use a fork to loosen any clumps so it will cook evenly. Replace the lid and complete the cooking time. You can make this dish on the stovetop, but using the rice cooker is faster and easier.

While the rice and meat are cooking, boil or steam the green beans until they are just tender.

Mix the Greek yogurt with the herbs and serve as a side dish with the beans.

Buffalo with Green Beans and Basmati Rice

Stuffed Eggplant

I once asked my grandmother why she made this dish once a year and only when it snowed. "Child," she said, "I told you more than once that eggplant is extremely hot, so I cook it in winter when your body can handle that much hot energy. Besides, it is not that easy to make. I'm old and tired. Now go play and don't bother me." Now that I am doing the cooking, I see what my grandmother meant. The preparation is time consuming, but it's worth it. I only cook this for very special occasions, and it always reminds me of her.

2 to 4 servings

1 large eggplant, peeled

1 large onion, chopped fine

1 clove garlic, chopped

3 tablespoons grapeseed oil

2 cups beef, ground

salt and pepper, to taste

2 tablespoons tomato paste

1/2 teaspoon turmeric

1 tablespoon fennel seeds

1 teaspoon fresh rosemary, chopped

1/2 cup cheddar cheese, grated

2 pieces pita bread, toasted

Preheat oven to 400°.

Slice off the top of the eggplant and scoop out the seeds and pulp with a spoon, being careful not to break it. Set aside.

In a medium-size frying pan, cook the onion and garlic in 2 tablespoons of the grapeseed oil. When they are soft, add the meat and mix well. Stir in the salt, pepper, tomato paste, turmeric, and fennel seeds. Add 1 cup of hot water and cook for 15 to 20 minutes. Set aside to cool.

Rub some oil on the eggplant, inside and out. With a spoon, stuff the eggplant with the meat mixture. Sprinkle rosemary and some cheese on top. Replace the eggplant top and roast in a small, high-sided baking pan or casserole dish for 40 minutes. Serve with toasted pita bread.

was living in Melbourne, which I call the "city of arts" because of all the art galleries and beautiful cafés on every corner. I worked in a restaurant for a while and created this very popular dish.

6 servings

1/2 cup coconut flour

1/4 cup almond meal

1 cup oats

1 pound beef, ground

1 teaspoon turmeric

3 tablespoons soy sauce

salt and pepper, to taste

1 tablespoon tomato paste

1 large onion, sliced thin

2 cloves garlic, crushed

3 tablespoons grapeseed oil

1 cup mushrooms, chopped

1 red bell pepper, chopped

1 small sweet potato, peeled and sliced thin

1 tablespoon fresh lime juice

Preheat oven to 400°.

Combine coconut flour, almond meal, oats, ground beef, turmeric, 1 tablespoon of the soy sauce, salt, pepper, and tomato paste in a large bowl. Using your hands, mix it well. Place mixture on a rectangular baking sheet and shape into a loaf. Cover with aluminum foil and bake for 45 to 50 minutes.

While the meat loaf is baking, fry the onion and garlic in the grapeseed oil. When they are soft, add mushrooms, bell pepper, and sweet potato. Add the lime juice, the remaining soy sauce, and salt and pepper to taste.

Remove meat loaf from oven when it's done, and let it cool down for 15 minutes. Transfer it gently to a deep platter, surround it with the vegetables, and pour the juice from the meat loaf over all. Serve with a garden salad and bread, if you wish.

Lamb Stew with Okra and Sweet Potato

O kra is an amazing vegetable. Unfortunately we don't use it as often as we should in the US. Its high fiber content is beneficial to the digestive system. It's loaded with antioxidants and vitamins C, K, and A as well as magnesium, all of which make a big contribution to good health. The vitamin B in okra is essential for pregnant women because it aids in the production and maintenance of new cells. Try to add this power-packed vegetable to your diet at least once a week.

The combination of okra, lamb, and sweet potato create balanced hot energy, which keeps you satisfied and gives you lots of energy through the day.

4 servings

2 tablespoons grapeseed oil

1/2 pound fresh okra

1 large red onion, chopped

1 pound lamb, cut into small pieces

1 teaspoon turmeric

salt and pepper, to taste

1 teaspoon curry powder

1 clove garlic, crushed

1 large sweet potato, cut into small pieces

1 tablespoon tomato paste

3 cups hot water

2 cups rice, steamed (see basic rice recipe page 30)

2 pieces pita bread, optional

Heat 1 tablespoon of the grapeseed oil and sauté the okra until it is browning and soft. Set aside.

In a medium-size pot, heat the remaining oil and sauté the onion and the lamb, breaking it up with a wooden spoon. Add the turmeric, salt, pepper, curry powder, and garlic. Cook a little longer to combine flavors, then add the sweet potato. Cook over medium heat, and when the meat and onion turn to golden brown, add the tomato paste and stir. Pour in the hot water, cover, and cook over medium heat for 45 to 50 minutes. Taste for doneness and seasoning, then add the okra and cook another 10 to 15 minutes.

Serve with steamed rice and pita bread, if you wish.

3 servings

5 cups water

1 tablespoon salt

2 tablespoons olive oil

1 cup rice noodles

6 lamb cutlets, trimmed of fat

salt and pepper, to taste

1/2 teaspoon turmeric

1 tablespoon soy sauce

1 teaspoon honey

2 tablespoons fresh lime or lemon juice

2 tablespoons avocado oil

1 cup mushrooms, sliced

1 cup cherry tomatoes

1/2 cup fresh cilantro, for garnish

1 tablespoon grapeseed or garlic oil, roasted

Bring water to a boil. Add salt and oil. Turn the burner off, then add the noodles to the pot, cover, and let them sit for 5 minutes. Drain the noodles and rinse with cold water. Shake the sieve a few times and set the noodles aside to dry.

In a large bowl, combine cutlets, salt, pepper, turmeric, soy sauce, honey, lime or lemon juice, and avocado oil. Use your hand to mix gently. Heat a frying pan to high heat and add the cutlets. Cook 3 to 5 minutes on each side. Transfer to a plate, cover, and set aside.

In the same pan, cook the mushrooms using 1 tablespoon of grapeseed or garlic oil for 3 to 5 minutes. Add the cherry tomatoes and cook for another 2 minutes.

Transfer the reserved noodles to a serving platter and sprinkle with salt and pepper. Arrange cutlets, cherry tomatoes, and mushrooms around them. Pour the juice from the pan over all and garnish with cilantro.

Lamb Chops with Mushrooms and Cherry Tomatoes

Chicken
and Turkey
Main Dishes

Fresh Cilantro Turkey and Chicken Patties

Every summer, during the school holiday, my grandmother and I went to live with my great aunty and her family on their big farm. There were fields covered with sunflowers and an orchard with cherry, apple, and orange trees. Lots of people worked on the farm, so every day, my aunty cooked for them, and at least once a week, my grandmother prepared this delicious meal.

I tried to create the same dish with a few changes, like the added turkey meat. The patties are made with low-fat, cold-energy meats, but the turmeric and garlic raise the hot energy, making them just right for a light evening meal. The garlic and turmeric pack an anti-inflammatory punch. Inflammation is commonly pointed at as a hindrance to weight loss as well as a contributing factor in painful joints, so this dish is healthy in just about every way possible.

4 servings

1/2 pound turkey, ground

1/2 pound chicken, ground

2 cloves garlic, crushed

1 onion, sliced thin

salt and pepper, to taste

1 teaspoon rosemary

1 teaspoon thyme

1/2 teaspoon turmeric

1 teaspoon curry powder

3 tablespoons olive oil

juice of 1 lime or lemon, halved

1 red bell pepper, sliced

1 cup fresh cilantro, chopped

1 cup fresh parsley, chopped

1 cup Greek yogurt

In a bowl, combine the turkey, chicken, garlic, onion, salt, pepper, rosemary, thyme, turmeric, curry powder, and 1 tablespoon of the olive oil. Using your hands, mix well. Heat remaining 2 tablespoons of the olive oil in a frying pan. Shape the mixture into medium-size patties and cook them for about 5 minutes, flipping them once during the cooking time. Drizzle lemon or lime juice on top, and garnish with the red pepper and fresh herbs. Serve Greek yogurt on the side.

n Pakistan and India, it's almost impossible to find anything to eat that isn't highly spiced. As a Persian, I wasn't accustomed to cooking with curry and other hot spices. However, once I was introduced to curry and came to understand the benefits of all those aromatic, hot, delicious spices, I couldn't help myself. It's not only the flavor they bring to dishes but also the antioxidants and the hot energy they create in everything you make.

4 servings

2 pounds skinless
chicken thighs

1/2 teaspoon turmeric

1 tablespoon
curry powder

salt and pepper,
to taste

3 tablespoons olive oil

1 large red onion, sliced

3 cloves garlic, sliced

1 lemon or lime, halved

1 large red bell pepper,
sliced

1 jalapeño pepper,
sliced

1 cup mushrooms,
sliced

pita bread

1 cup Greek yogurt

Preheat the oven to 400°.

Rinse the chicken thighs and trim the ends, if you like. Combine all the ingredients in a bowl except the lemon or lime, pita bread, and Greek yogurt and mix well, using your hands. Squeeze 1/2 of lemon or lime into bowl. Transfer to a baking dish, cover with foil, and bake for 45 minutes. Uncover and cook for 20 minutes more. Garnish with remaining half of lemon or lime. Serve with pita bread and Greek yogurt.

Grilled Rosemary Chicken Livers with Zucchini

This dish is dedicated to my beautiful cousin, who had a heart condition and passed away a long time ago. We grew up together, and this was our favorite dish. However, each time we ate it, we got in trouble with my grandmother. If you cook chicken livers for a long time, they will become hard and chewy, so do not overcook. We kids always talked with our mouths full, hurrying to finish quickly so we could go and play. We choked on the liver every time and got sent to our room for punishment. Nevertheless this is still one of my favorite foods. I make it a little bit differently, but like my grandmother, I say to my son, "Eat slowly and don't talk with your mouth full."

While chicken is normally a cold-energy meat, the livers, like all organ meats, are hot-energy food. With the addition of cold-energy zucchini, a perfect balance is achieved. Zucchini is high in vitamins A and C, fiber, copper, thiamin, niacin, and other healthy nutrients.

4 servings

3 tablespoons olive oil

1 large onion, sliced

2 cloves garlic, minced

2 large zucchini, sliced into rounds

1 pound organic chicken livers

1 tablespoon fresh rosemary, chopped

1/2 teaspoon salt

1/2 teaspoon pepper

1/2 teaspoon curry powder

1/2 teaspoon paprika

juice of 1 lime or lemon

salt and pepper, to taste

Heat 1 tablespoon olive oil in a frying pan and cook the onion and garlic until soft. Transfer the onions and garlic to a plate and set aside.

Cook the zucchini in 1 tablespoon olive oil the same pan for 2 minutes on each side. Return the onions and garlic to the pan. Cover and set aside.

Rinse the chicken livers and cut them into bite-size pieces, removing any fat you see. Let the meat dry on a paper towel. Combine livers, rosemary, salt, pepper, curry powder, paprika, and 1 tablespoon of the olive oil in a bowl. Mix with your hands until nicely coated. Place the liver pieces in the frying pan with 1 tablespoon olive oil and cook for 7 to 8 minutes on medium to high heat if you prefer it well done. Check it after a few minutes of cooking if you enjoy liver cooked until the middle is barely pink.

Add chicken livers to the onion and garlic and toss. Drizzle fresh lime or lemon juice on top and season with salt and pepper.

Grilled Rosemary Chicken Livers with Zucchini

Grilled Chicken with Tomatoes and Herbed Greek Yogurt

When I was living in Pakistan as a refugee, I befriended an older woman who became like a mother to me. She comforted me when I needed her motherly wisdom, and she taught me the art of cooking with spices. Because of her, I developed an appreciation for spicy foods. This recipe is from my *ama jee*, which means "dear mom."

This dish is simple and healthy at the same time, with lots of cold energy and a touch of spice that provides hot energy. It's high in protein and low in fat and contains lots of vitamin C and calcium.

4 servings

2 skinless chicken breasts

3 tablespoons olive oil

1 teaspoon curry powder

1 tablespoon fresh lemon juice

1/2 teaspoon turmeric

1 teaspoon honey

salt and pepper, to taste

2 tomatoes, halved

1 hot pepper such as red or green chile or cayenne, preferably fresh

1 cup Greek yogurt

1 cup fresh mint and cilantro, chopped

fresh lime

Rinse the chicken breasts and slice them horizontally, which makes them thinner and shortens the cooking time. Marinate the chicken in a bowl with the 2 tablespoons olive oil, curry powder, lemon juice, turmeric, honey, salt, and pepper. Make sure the chicken is well coated, cover, and refrigerate for an hour or two.

Preheat the grill plate or outdoor grill and cook the chicken 2 to 5 minutes per side. Be careful not to overcook, or the chicken will end up being dry. Place the tomato halves and the chili pepper on the grill top at this time.

Combine the Greek yogurt, herbs, a squeeze of fresh lime, and salt and pepper to taste. Serve the chicken and tomatoes with the herbal yogurt and a garden salad.

Always use fresh hot peppers if you can get them. The dried ones have lost most of their valuable vitamins and minerals.

Grilled Chicken with Tomatoes and Herbed Greek Yogurt

Chicken Kebabs with Garlic-Onion Mashed Potatoes

Traditional Iranian shish kebabs are not everyday fare because they can be time consuming to prepare. To serve something similar at home as often as the family wants, I created tasty and easy-to-make chicken kebabs. Although chicken and potatoes are cold-energy foods, adding garlic and turmeric helps balance this meal. I've found that children love the novelty of the kebab skewers and green mashed potatoes. Plus, it's a perfect dinner to help them wind down.

2 servings

1 skinless, boneless chicken breast

4 tablespoons olive oil

1/2 teaspoon turmeric

2 tablespoons fresh lemon juice

salt and pepper, to taste

1 large onion

2 cloves garlic, crushed

5 cups water

2 potatoes, peeled and halved

pinch of turmeric powder

1 cup fresh herbs, chopped (any combination of parsley, cilantro, mint, or thyme)

wooden skewers

1 cup fresh mint, for garnish

Rinse the chicken breast and cut into thin strips 3 to 4 inches long. This ensures the chicken is cooked thoroughly. In a large bowl, combine chicken, 3 tablespoons olive oil, turmeric, lemon juice, salt, and pepper, mixing well to coat the chicken. I prefer to use my hands for this task. If you do, be sure to wash your hands with soap and water afterwards. Cover and refrigerate for approximately 1 hour.

While the chicken is marinating, fry the onion and garlic in 1 tablespoon olive oil until they are golden brown. Add water to medium-size pan, heat to a boil, and put the potatoes in. When the potatoes are tender, drain and transfer to a bowl with salt and pepper to taste, a pinch of turmeric, the onion-and-garlic mixture, and the freshly chopped herbs. Blend to desired consistency.

Place the chicken strips on skewers to form kebabs. Grill or broil in the oven, 4 minutes on each side.

Serve the chicken kebabs on the skewers with the mashed potatoes on the side, garnishing with mint.

Chicken Kebabs with Garlic-Onion Mashed Potatoes

Oven-Baked Orange-Herb Chicken

This is a dish with loads of cold energy and hot flavor. Although thighs are dark meat, they still provide relaxing cold energy. The oranges offer cold energy too. The rosemary, cumin, and paprika give the dish the hot energy it needs for balance. Choose your side dishes based on whether you want to feel energized, want to wind down at the end of a long day, or seek the even energy in between. For more energy, serve it with brown rice. For smooth or even energy, serve fruit and brown rice on the side, and to relax, opt for mashed potatoes.

4 servings

2 pounds skinless chicken thighs

juice of 2 oranges

1 tablespoon orange zest

1 tablespoon honey

1 tablespoon paprika

1 tablespoon cumin powder

1 tablespoon fresh rosemary, chopped

juice of 1/2 lemon

1 tablespoon soy sauce

2 tablespoons olive oil

salt and pepper, to taste

orange slices

fresh mint, cilantro, or parsley, chopped

Preheat oven to 400°.

Combine chicken thighs, orange juice, orange zest, honey, paprika, cumin powder, rosemary, lemon juice, soy sauce, and olive oil in a bowl and mix well. Transfer to an ovenproof dish and cover with a lid or aluminum foil. Bake for 45 minutes. Remove the cover or aluminum foil and bake for another 30 to 45 minutes.

Serve with orange slices and, if you wish, sprinkle fresh chopped herbs such as mint, cilantro, or parsley on top.

This humble meal brings back lots of memories. We were living in Australia, and my daughter had just started going to school. I made her a sandwich like this for lunch almost every day. One day she asked me if she could please be "like other Australian kids and have a normal sandwich?" Of course I said yes! I think she meant white bread with cheddar cheese but I pretended I had no idea what she was talking about, and the next day, I added avocado and turkey breast to the sandwich.

This wrap has plenty of flavors and textures, so it's a crowd pleaser. That means that when you take it for lunch, you'll probably gather a crowd. The walnuts and avocados are both heart healthy and have lots of hot energy. The pita bread, turkey, and herbs all provide cold energy. Kids love to find this wrap in their lunch box, or when they come home hungry after school. The turkey is lean and high in protein, while the oil-rich avocado keeps you satisfied and feeling full until dinner.

2 servings

1 large avocado, sliced

10 slices 99% fat-free turkey breast

1 cup fresh cilantro, chopped

1/2 cup fresh dill, chopped

1 cup feta cheese

2 slices whole-grain pita bread

juice of 1 fresh lime

1 cup walnuts, crushed

fresh cilantro

Combine all the ingredients except the pita bread, walnuts, cilantro, and lime juice. Mix the ingredients well, then add the lime juice. Spoon the mixture onto the pita bread, roll it up gently, then wrap with plastic. Refrigerate for 1 hour. Cut the wraps into bite-size pieces, and serve with walnuts and fresh cilantro.

Avocado-Turkey Wrap with Walnuts

Turkey and Chicken Meatballs with Fresh Apple and Pear

So many mothers complain to me that their kids don't like to eat fresh fruits or vegetables, so I created this recipe. It's a delicious way for them to get their daily protein as well as fiber, minerals, calcium, vitamin C, and much more. The balance of hot and cold energy in this dish makes for a perfect dinner or light lunch if you want a relaxing afternoon. To lower the calories, bake the meatballs in the oven at 375° for 45 to 50 minutes instead of frying.

4 servings

1/2 pound turkey, minced

1/2 pound chicken, minced

1 cup fresh cilantro, chopped

1 cup fresh parsley, chopped

1/2 cup oats

1 clove garlic, minced

1/2 red onion, minced

1/2 teaspoon salt

1/2 teaspoon pepper

1/2 teaspoon turmeric

1/2 apple, unpeeled and grated

1/2 pear, unpeeled and grated

1 egg

1 cup grapeseed oil for cooking

fresh parsley or cilantro, chopped

Combine all the ingredients except the oil and herbs. Mix well. Form into small round balls with your hands. In a small saucepan, heat the grapeseed oil. When it is very hot, drop one ball into the hot oil at a time, and turn it gently. Deep-fry each meatball for 2 to 3 minutes, depending on their size. Garnish with chopped fresh parsley or cilantro and serve.

Sauce

1 medium onion, chopped in small pieces

3 tablespoons olive oil

2 cloves garlic, crushed and chopped in small pieces

1/2 teaspoon turmeric powder

salt and pepper, to taste

3 tablespoons tomato paste

3 cups hot water

1/2 cup fresh rosemary, thyme, and basil, chopped

In a medium size pot, cook onion and garlic in 3 tablespoons of olive oil over medium heat. Once onion starts to juice, add turmeric powder, salt, and pepper. Mix well, add 3 tablespoons tomato paste, and stir. Add 3 cups hot water and mix gently with a spoon. Lower the heat, add meatballs one by one, and then add fresh herbs. Cover and cook on low heat for 30 to 45 minutes. Sprinkle fresh herbs on top and serve.

Turkey and Chicken Meatballs with Fresh Apple and Pear

Honey Chicken with Grilled Vegetables

A Moroccan friend of mine often talked about the energy of food and how, in her culture, they revere the healing power of energy, curing illness by balancing the diet. Every time I make this chicken dish, I remember our conversations and the time we spent together.

This meal is sweet and tasty, with both hot and cold energy. Honey, which I fondly call the Queen of Sweetness, is a natural antibiotic with healing powers. Compared to other types of sugars, honey has also been shown to keep blood sugar levels fairly constant. This dish balances cold-energy chicken with hot-energy mushrooms and bell peppers. You can safely add a side dish or dessert with hot energy and enjoy the rest of your evening.

4 servings

2 pounds skinless chicken drumsticks

1/2 pound mushrooms, quartered

3 red and green bell peppers, cut into chunks

2 red onions, cut into chunks

1 clove garlic, crushed

salt and pepper, to taste

1 tablespoon tomato paste

2 tablespoons grapeseed oil

1 tablespoon honey

1/2 teaspoon turmeric

1/2 teaspoon curry powder

1 fresh tomato, cut into chunks

lemon, for garnish

Preheat oven to 400°.

Combine all the ingredients except lemon in a large bowl and mix with your hands. Transfer to an ovenproof dish and cover with a lid or aluminum foil. Bake for about 45 minutes. Uncover and bake for an additional 25 minutes or until the top has turned a nice shade of brown and not much liquid remains. Garnish with lemon. This dish goes very well with rice or with a green salad.

Honey Chicken with Grilled Vegetables

walked three or four kilometers to school every morning, then home for lunch, and back to school again in the afternoon. Altogether that added up to something like ten miles. As you can imagine, getting sick was like a blessing from God because then I could stay home and enjoy grandmother's chicken soup and listen to all her stories. Unfortunately, after half an hour or so, I would start running around, and she knew then that I was feeling all right. She'd send me to work in her vegetable garden, and I would wish I'd gone school.

Pumpkins are rich in minerals, and they contain cancer-fighting carotene. The ones with the deepest orange coloring have the most nutrients. The combination of the pumpkin (which is actually a cool-season squash), hot-energy garlic and red onions, and cold-energy chicken makes this soup a wonderfully balanced meal for summer or winter.

4 to 6 servings

1 small pumpkin, peeled, cleaned out, and cut into small pieces

salt and pepper, to taste

1 teaspoon turmeric

1 teaspoon olive oil

1 whole chicken, cooked

1 red onion, diced

1 cup low-sodium chicken stock

1 cup bean sprouts

1/2 cup fresh cilantro, chopped

1 lime, cut into wedges

Preheat oven to 400°.

Arrange the pumpkin pieces on a baking sheet, sprinkle salt, pepper, and turmeric over them, and drizzle olive oil on top. Toss to coat. Roast for 30 minutes.

Remove the skin and bones from the chicken and chop it into very small pieces. Heat a little bit of oil in a medium-size pot and cook the onion until golden brown. Add the chicken and cook for about 2 minutes.

When the pumpkin slices are tender, transfer them to a bowl and mash them. Add the mashed pumpkin and the chicken stock to the chicken. Combine well and cook on medium heat for about 10 minutes. Serve garnished with bean sprouts, cilantro, and lime wedges.

I add turmeric to most of my dishes because of its great healing powers. It does wonders for people with poor digestion, and its antioxidants and anti-inflammatory properties help alleviate joint pain from arthritis.

Pumpkin and Chicken Soup

Pumpkin and Chicken Soup

Toasted Turkey-Spinach Wrap

The hot energy of the egg and the cold energy of the turkey provide the balance you need in the middle of a busy day. All the ingredients not only complement each other on the energy spectrum but also provide a delicious combination.

4 servings

4 eggs

4 spinach tortillas

1 avocado,
sliced thin

1 large tomato,
sliced thin

4 or 8 slices turkey,
roasted

1 tablespoon olive oil

salt and pepper,
to taste

2 oranges, sliced

Fry the eggs in olive oil to your liking. Lay the tortillas out flat. Layer avocado slices, an egg, and tomato slices, ending with the turkey. Gently roll the tortillas into a firm wrap. Heat them in the frying pan or on a grill plate for 1 minute on each side. Serve with sliced orange or any other fruit.

Pure saffron, considered to be somewhat of an aphrodisiac, has been revered for thousands of years. It is expensive but is well worth it for the wonderful flavor and aroma it adds. This dish also features lemon, which is high in vitamin C, a natural immune-system booster.

4 servings

2 small whole chickens, giblets removed

3 tablespoons olive oil

salt and pepper, to taste

2 large oranges, halved

2 lemons, halved

2 large onions, diced

4 cloves garlic, chopped

1 tablespoon fennel seeds

1 tablespoon honey

pinch of saffron

1 cup fresh parsley, chopped

1 orange, sliced, for garnish

Preheat the oven to 400°.

Rinse the chickens and pat dry. Rub them with the olive oil and a little bit of salt and pepper. Cut an orange and lemon in half and squeeze the juice of an orange and a lemon over the chickens. Distribute the onion and garlic in the bottom of a high-sided roasting pan and place the chickens on top. Sprinkle some salt and pepper, fennel seeds, honey, and saffron as well as the juice from the rest of the lemon and orange halves over the chickens. Cover the pan with aluminum foil and roast in the oven for 45 minutes. Uncover and continue roasting until the tops of the birds are golden brown. Set the chickens on a platter and garnish with fresh parsley and orange slices.

Orange and Lemon Chicken with Saffron

Chicken Stuffed with Mushrooms and Feta Cheese

I once worked in a restaurant owned by a difficult person to please. I was a waitperson, but I really wanted to cook. I pestered him for a chance and promised I'd show him that I could cook, but he always rejected my pleas. Finally he got tired of hearing me say, "One chance, just give me one chance." He said, "I'll give you thirty minutes to make something elegant, fast, and tasty." When you taste this dish, you'll understand why it convinced him to hire me as an assistant chef.

I use plenty of hot-energy mushrooms to balance the very cold energy of the chicken, making this an ideal evening meal. Red bell peppers, which are mildly spicy, are also very rich in vitamin C. In fact, they have twice as much vitamin C as green peppers. They also contain lycopene, which fights cancer. The feta cheese in this dish adds a traditional Mediterranean taste.

4 servings

5 tablespoons olive oil

1 onion, diced

2 cloves garlic, crushed

1 cup mushrooms, halved

1 red bell pepper, diced

salt and pepper, to taste

pinch of paprika

2 teaspoons soy sauce

1 pound skinless, boneless chicken breasts

1 tablespoon dried oregano

1 tablespoon dried rosemary

1 tablespoon dried thyme

1 cup feta cheese

Heat 2 tablespoons olive oil and add the onion and garlic. When they are half cooked, add the mushrooms and bell pepper. When the vegetables are almost done, add salt, pepper, paprika, and soy sauce and continue cooking a few more minutes.

Rinse the chicken breasts and pat dry. Lay them on a cutting board and slice them so they are half the thickness. You may want to ask your butcher to do this for you. Spread the vegetables on the chicken breasts. Sprinkle the herbs and feta cheese over the top. Gently roll the breasts. If necessary, use toothpick to hold the rolls in place. Heat the remaining oil in the frying pan and cook the chicken rolls for 5 to 7 minutes on each side. Cover and continue to cook for a few more minutes. Set the rolls on a plate and pour the juices from the pan over them.

Chicken Stuffed with Mushrooms and Feta Cheese

Satay Chicken with Oranges and Cherry Tomatoes

While traveling through Malaysia, I enjoyed a chicken-and-rice dish so delicious I had to recreate it when I returned home to Australia. I simply made a few changes to balance the energy.

4 servings

2 cups brown rice

4 cups water

salt and pepper, to taste

3 tablespoons olive oil

1 large onion, sliced

1 clove garlic, crushed

1 skinless, boneless chicken breast, cut into strips

1/2 teaspoon turmeric

a few slices fresh ginger or 1 teaspoon ginger, ground

1 cup orange, peeled and cubed

1/2 cup cherry tomatoes, halved

1 tablespoon honey

1 tablespoon fresh lemon juice

1/2 cup fresh cilantro and basil, chopped

Rinse the rice and cook in water with a bit of salt and 1 tablespoon of olive oil.

Heat 2 tablespoons of the olive oil in a wok or a large frying pan. When the oil is hot, add the onion and garlic. After a few minutes, add the chicken strips, salt, pepper, turmeric, and ginger. Stir well and continue stirring often as they cook. When the chicken is almost done, add orange cubes, cherry tomatoes, honey, and lemon juice. Finish cooking, and add fresh herbs just before serving.

T he balanced cold energy of this dish is ideal for dinner. It's packed with protein, omega-3s, vitamin C, and fiber. Dried plums benefit the digestive system, keeping it in tip-top shape.

4 to 6 servings

2 tablespoons olive oil

1 pound skinless chicken breasts or drumsticks

2 garlic gloves, crushed

1 large onion, chopped

1 teaspoon ginger, ground

1 teaspoon turmeric

salt and pepper, to taste

3 cups hot water

1 large potato, peeled and cubed

1 cup of dried plums (prunes), rinsed

3 cups basmati rice

1/2 teaspoon saffron powder

Heat 2 tablespoons of the olive oil in a large pot with a lid. Add the chicken, garlic, onion, and ginger. When the onion releases its juices and turns golden brown, add the turmeric, salt, and pepper and stir with a wooden spoon. Add the hot water, cover, and cook for about 20 minutes on medium heat. Add the potato and dried plums. Check for salt and add more, if necessary. It's important to take tastes as you cook so you don't end up with a dish that's too salty or has no taste at all. Cook another 30 minutes, checking periodically to see if there is enough water in the pot. This dish should not be too runny but should have enough juices to make it moist and flavorful.

While the chicken is cooking, make the rice (see basic rice recipe on page 30). Stir the saffron powder in 1 tablespoon of hot water and add it to the cooked rice, incorporating it gently with a fork. Sometimes, instead of rice, you may want to serve this dish with pita bread or a tossed salad.

Saffron Chicken with Dried Plums and Potatoes

Fesenjoon (Chicken Cooked with Crushed Walnuts and Pomegranate Molasses)

My grandmother never cooked this dish in the summer because she believed it had too much hot energy. During winter, our bodies can handle it, and in fact, it helps balance the energy. Nowadays I don't worry so much about too much hot energy. I can always balance it by adding cold-energy yogurt to the meal.

My grandmother always recommended this dish to young couples who wanted to start a family. "If you want to have a child, feed your husband *fesenjoon*," she said.

Fesenjoon has lots of omega-3s, protein, phosphorous, and antioxidants. The pomegranate molasses contributes more antioxidants plus a host of B vitamins. It also helps your body to produce more energy and keeps your heart healthy. With all its hot energy, *fesenjoon* is best served at lunch; otherwise, your family will have a difficult time going to sleep.

4 to 6 servings

2 tablespoons olive oil

1 large onion, chopped

1/2 teaspoon turmeric

2 cups walnuts

4 cups of warm water

salt and pepper, to taste

3 tablespoons brown or raw sugar

6 tablespoons pomegranate molasses

1 pound skinless chicken drumsticks

2 cups basmati rice

1/4 teaspoon saffron powder

1 cup fresh cilantro, chopped, for garnish

2 cups Greek yogurt

Heat the olive oil in a large pot and sauté the onion with the turmeric. Stir to keep it from burning.

While the onion is cooking, put the walnuts in a blender, one cup at a time, and grind them to a very fine consistency. There should be no chunks. The texture is almost like a pureé.

Add the ground walnuts to the onion and stir to mix well. Add 4 cups of warm water, salt, pepper, brown sugar, and molasses. Stir again to mix well and cover. Cook on low heat for at least an hour. Check every 10 minutes and stir to keep it from burning. Taste for sweetness. Add sugar if desired, but remember, the level of sweetness should be like molasses, which is not as sweet as sugar.

Rinse the drumsticks and cook them over medium heat in a pan without oil. Cook for 5 to 7 minutes until they begin to brown. Transfer them to the pot with the walnut mixture when that has been cooking for about 30 minutes. After cooking for an hour, the mixture should have thickened somewhat. It shouldn't be runny. I promise, if you follow the directions, this will be delicious. It's very different from any dish you've ever tasted.

Cook the rice (see basic rice recipe on page 30). Just before serving it, mix the saffron powder with 1 tablespoon of hot water. Pour it over the rice and mix it gently with a fork.

Transfer the rice to a large platter and heap the chicken on top. Garnish with the chopped cilantro and serve with Greek yogurt on the side.

Walnuts are thought to have a positive effect on testosterone levels. In addition to the occasional fesenjoon, you might want to add a handful of walnuts to your husband's daily diet.

Fesenjoon (Chicken Cooked with Crushed Walnuts and Pomegranate Molasses)

Seafood
Main Dishes

Citrus-Flavored Seafood Platter

This is another dish I created while I was living in Australia. Seafood was quite pricey back then, as it is now, so I only made this for special occasions. One of my girlfriends got the recipe from me and made it for her boyfriend. They ended up getting married, and I can't help but think my recipe had something to do with it.

Though the seafood and lime are cold energy—ideal for an evening meal—the ginger and paprika balance the dish with their hot energy. Ginger is believed to lower cholesterol as well as relieve joint inflammation, which can trigger allergies and arthritis. I always recommend it for upset stomachs and headaches. Grate a small amount into a steaming cup of hot water and let it steep.

4 servings

4 tablespoons olive oil

4 cloves garlic, minced

1 red onion, sliced thin

1 tablespoon fresh ginger, grated

1 fresh tomato, diced

salt and pepper, to taste

1/2 teaspoon turmeric

2 oranges, for zest and juice

1/2 tablespoon paprika

1 cup fresh parsley, chopped

10 cups water

1 lobster tail, cut in half, shell on

1 pound mussels

1/4 cup garlic oil, roasted

1/2 pound prawns or shrimp, peeled

1 red bell pepper, diced

2 limes, cut into wedges

Heat 3 tablespoons olive oil and add the garlic, onion, and ginger. When the onions are soft, stir in the tomato, salt, pepper, turmeric, and grated orange peel or zest.

Combine 1 tablespoon olive oil, paprika, orange juice, and fresh parsley in a small bowl and mix well.

Bring 10 cups water, or until the pot is half full, to a boil in a medium-size pot. Drop in the lobster halves and cook 4 to 5 minutes, or until they turn pink. Transfer to a colander to drain and cool. Put the mussels in the same pot of boiling water. Cook until the shells open. Drain and transfer to the colander. Discard any mussels that did not open. In a frying pan, heat roasted garlic oil and cook the prawns until they turn pink, then continue cooking for 3 to 5 more minutes. Set aside to cool.

Combine the seafood in a large bowl. Add the vegetables and the orange sauce. Mix well. Squeeze some fresh lime juice on top for more zest.

Citrus-Flavored Seafood Platter

Sweet and Spicy Mussels with Lime

I lived for a time on the island of Tasmania, in the beautiful city of Hobart. It was here that I met my first Australian friend, a fellow student. After twenty years, she and I are still good friends. Tasmania has the best and the freshest seafood I ever tasted. It inspired me to create this and other scrumptious dishes while I was living there. It is dedicated to all my "Tessie" friends.

This recipe is balanced, but it provides an abundance of cool energy. All seafood, except tuna, is cold, and that is why it has such a wonderful calming influence. While most of the ingredients of this recipe make it spicy, which is hot energy, the cold energy of the mussels takes charge. I love that cilantro has been traditionally used in Latin America to soothe stomach upsets. Remember, cilantro's flavor diminishes with prolonged heat. Keep that it mind when you use this cool-energy herb in this and other recipes.

2 servings

1 pound mussels

3 tablespoons olive oil

2 cloves garlic, minced

1 onion, sliced thin

1 red bell pepper, chopped

1 cup mushrooms, sliced thin

1 teaspoon paprika

1/2 tablespoon dried chili pepper

1/2 teaspoon turmeric

1 tablespoon honey

salt and pepper, to taste

1/2 cup fresh cilantro, chopped

1/2 cup fresh parsley, chopped

2 limes

cabbage leaves

lime slices

Scrub and rinse the mussels. Drop them into a pot of boiling water and cook for about 4 to 5 minutes. Drain and set aside. Discard any mussels that didn't open during the cooking.

Heat the olive oil in a frying pan over medium heat and toss in the garlic, onion, bell pepper, and mushrooms. When these are tender, stir in the paprika, dried chili pepper, turmeric, honey, salt, and pepper. Add the mussels and fresh herbs to the pan and stir again. Squeeze lime juice over the top.

Serve on cabbage leaves and garnish with lime slices.

Shrimp Kebabs

This dish is great as an entrée, but it's also simple enough to serve as a light snack or appetizer. I love the way the honey and the lemon complement each other, and the strawberry garnish adds even more appeal. The shrimp, strawberries, and lemon have cold energy, but the olive oil and garlic contribute hot energy to balance the dish.

2 servings

1 pound shrimp

juice of 1 lemon

4 tablespoons olive oil

3 cloves garlic, crushed

1 teaspoon honey

1 tablespoon soy sauce

salt and pepper, to taste

1 lime, halved

1 cup fresh strawberries, sliced

Peel the shrimp, leaving the tails. Combine the shrimp, lemon juice, olive oil, garlic, honey, soy sauce, salt, and pepper in a large bowl. Mix with your hands. Spear shrimp on skewers, or wait until after they are cooked, whichever you prefer. Preheat the grill plate on high and grill the shrimp until they turn pink and are cooked through. Drizzle with fresh lime juice and serve with strawberries.

Seafood Cutlet

Working at the restaurant in Tasmania taught me to be creative and come up with new ideas every day. The owner was very open-minded. "To be a chef, you have to think like an artist," he often said. "Every day, I want you to be more creative than yesterday. Make something that not only tastes good but looks so gorgeous the customers will want to take a picture before they eat it."

This dish would definitely have pleased him. It is low in fat and high in protein, vitamin C, potassium, and iron. Though the egg, chili pepper, and turmeric add some hot energy, this is primarily a cold-energy dish, which helps you relax. That's why I recommend it as an excellent meal for the end of your day.

2 servings

1 cup shrimp, cooked, peeled and chopped

1 can water-packed wild salmon or tuna, drained

1 cup fresh cilantro, chopped

1 cup fresh dill, chopped

1 fresh red chili pepper, chopped

1 cup quick oats

turmeric, to taste

1 egg

1 red bell pepper, half chopped and half sliced

1 lime, halved

salt and pepper, to taste

3 tablespoons olive oil

fresh spinach

Combine the shrimp, salmon or tuna, cilantro, dill, chili pepper, oats, turmeric, egg, half of the red bell pepper (chopped), juice of one lime half, salt, and pepper. Thoroughly mix all of these ingredients with your hands. Form patties. Heat the olive oil in a frying pan and cook the patties 4 to 5 minutes on each side. Drizzle juice of lime half and olive oil on top and serve with fresh spinach and sliced red bell pepper.

Light and Tasty Salmon

I have a friend whose family doesn't like the smell of seafood, so she never cooks fish for them. I told her to let me cook dinner one night, and sure enough, the mission was accomplished. After tasting this dish, they understood that it is just a matter of using the right spices and herbs. Now they love light and tasty salmon.

Salmon, which is a cold-water fish, gives you plenty of cold energy, so it's perfect for dinner.

2 servings

1/2 teaspoon salt

1/2 teaspoon black pepper

1/2 teaspoon paprika

1/2 teaspoon turmeric

pinch of saffron powder

1/2 cup fresh dill, chopped

1 teaspoon flaxseed

1/2 teaspoon cumin powder

1 egg

1 cup unbleached flour

2 tablespoons grapeseed oil

2 salmon filets, 1/2 pound each

1 tablespoon fresh lime juice

1 fresh lemon, sliced, for garnish

fresh dill, for garnish

Combine salt, pepper, paprika, turmeric, saffron powder, dill, flaxseed, cumin powder, egg, and flour in a large bowl and mix well to create the seasoned coating. Remove the skin of the salmon filets and dip both sides in the seasoned coating. Heat the grapeseed oil in a frying pan. Fry the coated salmon filets 4 minutes on each side. Cook longer for a crunchier texture. Drizzle lime juice on top and garnish with sliced lemon and fresh dill.

Grilled Snapper with Fresh Strawberries

When I was living with my grandmother, I only saw my father occasionally and then just for a few hours at a time. If he was in a good mood, he took me fishing. He was not a very good fisherman, and though he never caught anything, he tried to fool me into thinking that he did.

On the way home, he always stopped at a fish market. "Wait here," he would tell me. "I will be back in a second." He inevitably returned with a huge fish—very similar to snapper—and pretended he had caught it but had left it in his friend's creel and just got it back. I knew the truth, but I wanted to spend time with him, and I wanted to believe my father was a great fisherman, so I always humored him, saying, "Wow! Let me look at it!" Whenever I cook snapper, it reminds me of my father and those few hours we spent together.

Snapper, like almost all fish, is cold energy. It provides the important fats that we need in our diets. It's a perfect summer meal and looks beautiful on the platter. Strawberries, which are also cold energy, add a tangy flavor in addition to some vitamin C. I add the herbs, in particular the dill, to balance the dish with some hot energy.

4 servings

4 snapper filets

1 teaspoon salt

1 teaspoon pepper

2 fresh limes

2 tablespoons olive oil

1 cup fresh strawberries, sliced

1 cup fresh dill, chopped

Gently rinse the filets and lay in a deep ovenproof dish. Sprinkle the salt and pepper and squeeze the juice of 1 lime over the filets. Drizzle 2 tablespoons olive oil over them and rub it in, making sure they're well coated. In a frying pan, heat 1 tablespoon of olive oil and fry the fish for 3 minutes on each side or until they are cooked to your taste. You can also grill the fish or cook it in the oven at 400° for 15 to 25 minutes, depending on the thickness of the filets. Serve the strawberries on the side with the fresh dill.

Hot Soup with Cool Energy

Tasmania is a beautiful place with a wonderful climate that reminds me of northern Iran, but while I lived there, we had one of the coldest winters on record. I got up early every morning and made this delicious soup for my daughter. I couldn't always afford to add shrimp, but even without it, the soup tasted great. As we ate it, we started to sweat. Its spiciness kept us warm for a long time.

The ingredients of this delicious soup create cool energy even though there are added hot ingredients such as the mushrooms and garlic. You can add more hot-energy foods to balance by substituting the rice noodles, which are cold energy, with egg noodles, which are hotter in nature. You can turn up the heat even more by adding chopped fresh ginger and chilis. I turn it into the perfect hot-energy breakfast for my son by poaching an egg, which is hot energy, and adding it to the soup. He loves to eat this before school. Although it's not traditional to eat soup for breakfast, you can imagine how comforting and filling it is to begin the day with warm soup on a cool morning.

2 servings

1 teaspoon olive oil

4 or 5 spring onions, sliced thin

1 clove garlic

1 cup shiitake mushrooms, sliced thin

4 cups water

salt

1 cup rice noodles

3 cups organic chicken stock

1 teaspoon fish sauce

1 teaspoon soy sauce

1 cup cauliflower, cut into small pieces

1 pound jumbo shrimp, peeled

1 fresh lime

1 cup fresh cilantro, chopped

Heat the olive oil in a medium-size pot. Add the onion, garlic, and mushrooms and cook for about 5 minutes.

Bring a pot of water to boil with a bit of salt and oil, and cook the rice noodles for a maximum of 2 to 3 minutes. Drain and rinse under cold water to stop the cooking. Drain again and shake the sieve so they will dry faster.

Add chicken stock, fish sauce, and soy sauce to the mushrooms and onions. Cook for 5 to 10 more minutes. Add the cauliflower and shrimp and cook for several more minutes.

Just before serving, add the noodles to the shrimp mixture. Squeeze lime juice over all and garnish with cilantro.

Hot Soup with Cool Energy

Fish Kebabs

A long time ago, I worked as a nanny for a very wealthy family. The three children were very fussy eaters, so I created many dishes the kids loved. No doubt, those colorful, healthy, fast, and easy dishes helped me keep my job.

The fish and rice of this dish are cold energy, but the meal is completely balanced by the hot energy of the herbs and the pineapple. If your children aren't fond of fish, let them try this dish. They will love the fun skewers and the sweetness of the pineapple. Notice how colorful this dish is. Bright colors in foods, like the red in the bell peppers and the yellow of the pineapple, signal a wealth of antioxidants.

2 to 4 servings

2 salmon or swordfish filets, 1/2 pound each, cubed

1 cup fresh pineapple, cubed

juice of 1/2 lime

1 large red bell pepper, chopped

salt and pepper, to taste

1/2 teaspoon turmeric

3 tablespoons olive oil

2 cups rice

1 cup fresh cilantro, chopped

wooden skewers

fresh lime or lemon, for garnish

Combine the fish, pineapple, the juice of half a lime, half of the red bell pepper, salt, pepper, turmeric, and olive oil in a large bowl and mix with your hands. Refrigerate while you prepare the rice.

Prepare the rice (see basic rice recipe on page 30) Add the cilantro and remaining red bell pepper to the cooked rice.

Preheat the grill plate or set oven to broil. Alternate pieces of fish, pineapple, and pepper on the wooden skewers. Set the skewers on a grilling tray or a shallow roasting pan if you are using the oven. Cook about 4 minutes on each side. Serve with the rice and garnish with a fresh lime or lemon.

This makes a perfect evening meal thanks to its balanced cold energy. It contains lots of omega-3s, protein, and good fats, all the things that are important for brain health.

2 servings

2 salmon filets	3 tablespoons olive oil
salt and pepper, to taste	2 cups mushrooms, sliced thin
1/2 teaspoon turmeric	1 cup bok choy, chopped
1/2 teaspoon caraway seeds, ground	1/2 avocado, sliced lengthwise
juice of 1 lime or lemon	

Rinse salmon filets and pat dry. Combine salt, pepper, turmeric, caraway seeds, and 1/2 of the lime or lemon juice. Gently coat the fish with this mixture and set aside to marinate for at least 30 minutes, a few hours if possible.

Heat a grill plate or frying pan, brush it with 1 tablespoon olive oil, and when the oil is hot, cook the filets for 3 to 5 minutes on each side. Don't overcook as this will rob them of their good flavor.

Heat 1 tablespoon of olive oil in another frying pan and cook the mushrooms for 2 to 3 minutes. Transfer to a plate. Cook the bok choy in the same pan. The vegetables should still be a little bit crunchy, not overcooked.

Arrange the salmon and the vegetables on a plate and serve with sliced avocado. Drizzle fresh lime juice and the remaining tablespoon of olive oil over the top and serve.

Grilled Salmon with Bok Choy and Mushrooms

Grilled Salmon and Mango Salad

This is another beautiful dish I created when I was a nanny. The children had a very strict diet—no pork, red meats, sweets, or junk foods. To keep from losing my job, I had to prepare foods that were healthy and also beautiful, fun, and interesting for those kids, tempting them to eat. It was quite a challenge. Every night after work, I went home and thought about new dishes I could cook for them. Like a painter faced with a blank canvas, I stared at a white plate until inspiration hit. Then I went to my pantry, assembled the ingredients, and created the next masterpiece for those fussy eaters.

This dish is light and flavorful, with perfect balance. The salmon offers cold energy, and the mangos provide hot energy. Mangos are a great source of vitamin C, carotene, copper, and B vitamins. The chickpeas (also known as garbanzo beans) are rich in protein. This dish will help you relax and put you in a good mood. Note that dill is hot, so if you use a lot of dill in this dish, the energy will shift from calming to neutral.

2 servings

2 salmon or red snapper filets

salt and pepper, to taste

1 tablespoon paprika

juice of 1 lemon

3 tablespoons olive oil

1 large mango, sliced thin

1 cup chickpeas, cooked

1 cup fresh dill, chopped

1 cup cherry tomatoes

1 cup mixed greens

small red onion, sliced very thin

1 tablespoon balsamic vinegar

1 teaspoon Dijon mustard

lemon wedges, for garnish

Lay the fish on a plate. Sprinkle salt, pepper, and paprika, then drizzle lemon juice and 1 tablespoon of the olive oil over the top. Set aside.

Combine mango, cooked chickpeas, dill, cherry tomatoes, mixed greens, and onion in a bowl. Toss with the remaining 2 tablespoons olive oil, 1 tablespoon lemon juice, balsamic vinegar, Dijon mustard, and salt and pepper.

Heat the grill plate, brush it with olive oil, and cook the salmon 3 to 4 minutes on each side or until done. Flake the fish into small pieces and add to the salad. Garnish with lemon wedges.

Grilled Salmon and Mango Salad

Zucchini Pasta with Grilled Mahi-Mahi

By the time I gave birth to my son, I had gained 28 pounds. I didn't want to go to extremes to lose all that extra weight. Instead, I wanted to do it by balancing the amount of hot and cold energy I gave my body. At the same time, because I was breastfeeding, I had to consider my son's nutritional needs, so I created many healthy and energy-balanced meals like this one.

This dish's cold energy promotes calm and relaxation. It is low in calories and high in minerals, potassium, vitamin A, manganese, and omega-3s. It's a cooling dish on a hot summer day.

4 servings

3 mahi-mahi filets

1 medium zucchini, sliced into long strips

salt and pepper, to taste

3 tablespoons olive oil

1/2 teaspoon turmeric

1 tablespoon red wine vinegar

juice of 1 fresh lime or lemon

1/2 cup fresh thyme and rosemary, chopped

Rinse the fish and pat dry. Cut it into small pieces.

Combine zucchini strips, salt, pepper, 1 tablespoon of the olive oil, turmeric, and red wine vinegar. Mix well but gently so the zucchini strips don't break.

In another bowl, combine the fish, salt and pepper to taste, 1/2 of the lime or lemon juice, and 1 tablespoon of the olive oil. Mix gently. Heat up the grill pan, brush with 1 tablespoon olive oil, and cook the fish for 2 to 3 minutes on each side. Transfer to a plate, cover, and set aside.

On the same grill plate, cook the zucchini strips for 2 to 3 minutes. Transfer to the plate with the fish. Drizzle the remaining lemon or lime juice and olive oil over all and garnish with fresh chopped rosemary and thyme or sprinkle them on top.

2 servings

1/2 package spaghetti

3 tablespoons grapeseed oil

1 medium onion, chopped

1 cup mushrooms, thinly sliced

1 cup cherry tomatoes, halved

salt and pepper, to taste

1/2 teaspoon turmeric

1/2 teaspoon curry powder

1/2 teaspoon fennel seeds

juice of 1 fresh lemon

1 salmon or tuna filet

1 tablespoon olive oil

1/2 cup fresh dill, chopped

Cook spaghetti in boiling water with salt and little bit of oil. Drain and rinse with cold water. Set aside in a large bowl.

Heat 1 tablespoon of the grapeseed oil in a frying pan and add onion. After a few minutes of cooking, add mushrooms and cook for another 3 to 4 minutes. Add cherry tomatoes and cook for 2 minutes. Pour over the reserved spaghetti. Sprinkle with salt and pepper and toss gently using two forks. Cover and set aside.

Combine salt, pepper, turmeric, curry powder, fennel seeds, lemon juice, and remaining 2 tablespoons of the grapeseed oil in a bowl. Add fish and mix, coating the fish with the marinade. Heat up a frying pan and cook the fish for 3 minutes on each side.

Flake the fish into small pieces with a fork and add to the spaghetti. Drizzle with olive oil and some lemon juice. Sprinkle with salt and pepper, and if you wish, garnish with fresh chopped dill.

Sweets

Baklava Cake

When I was a child growing up in Iran, people never called to let you know they were coming to visit. They just showed up, usually after lunch or dinner. Now everybody's lives are much busier. People still like to visit, but they call first. In Iran or any Middle Eastern country, guests are considered a blessing, and no one is turned away.

My grandmother reserved baklava cake for special occasions and for surprise guests. She stored it in the refrigerator so she would always have something on hand. She laid down the law in our household: "This baklava is just for guests!" She meant "don't you dare touch it," but of course, I always did. I didn't mind the punishment as long as I could eat my fill of delicious baklava cake.

This cake is my version of the traditional Mediterranean treat. Dense and rich, it has plenty of hot energy. The apples and oranges in this recipe add a hint of cold energy, but the nuts, sweeteners, and spices are all hot energy. This is a great afternoon treat when you have a lot to do.

6 to 8 servings

3 cinnamon sticks

10 whole cardamom seeds

1 red apple, chopped

2 large oranges and the zest of one

3 cups brown sugar

1/2 cup walnuts, ground

1/2 cup almonds, ground

1/2 cup pistachios, ground

1/2 cup cashews, ground

1/2 cup pecans, ground

2 cups unbleached flour

1 1/2 teaspoons baking soda

pinch of salt

1 teaspoon cardamom, ground

1 teaspoon cinnamon, ground

5 eggs

3 tablespoons olive oil

5 tablespoons rosewater

1 teaspoon lemon zest

honey, to taste

Preheat oven to 375°.

Grease a round cake pan with olive oil.

Combine 3 cups of water, cinnamon sticks, cardamom seeds, 1/2 chopped apple, and the skin of 1 orange in a pot and set on low heat. After simmering for about 45 minutes, add 1 cup of the brown sugar and stir periodically, making sure it does not burn. When most of the water has evaporated and the mixture has thickened, turn off the heat and let it cool. Once the mixture has cooled, pour it through a sieve and set aside.

Mix the nuts in a blender. In a large bowl, combine 2 cups of the brown sugar, the nut mixture, flour, baking soda, salt, ground cardamom, and ground cinnamon. Set aside.

Mix the eggs, olive oil, and rosewater with an electric mixer for 2 minutes. Fold the cooled orange and spice syrup into the egg mixture, then gently fold in the zest of 1 orange and the lemon zest.

Add the liquid ingredients to the dry ingredients and blend with an electric mixer for 3 to 4 minutes. If the mixture is too thick, add more rosewater or orange juice.

Pour the batter into the cake pan. Sprinkle some crushed nuts and drizzle some honey on top. Shake the pan or tap it gently on the counter a few times to release the air bubbles. Bake for 40 to 50 minutes. Cool for 15 to 20 minutes before serving with tea or coffee.

Rosewater is a very common ingredient in Middle Eastern cooking and baking. Because of its pleasant aroma and cooling effect, it is also a popular refreshing beverage. You can find rose, mint, dill, and orange blossom waters in Indian and Persian markets.

Baklava Cake

Spicy Nut Cake

My love of spicy food led me to create this spicy cake that tingles a bit on the tongue and is full of goodness. It's well balanced, with hot energy from ginger, cayenne pepper, and nuts to keep your energy level high for a long time. It's packed with essential minerals, protein, iron, potassium, and good fats to help the body function properly.

6 to 8 servings

4 eggs

2 cups brown sugar

1 cup grapeseed oil

4 cups self-rising flour

1 tablespoon fresh ginger, grated

2 cups almonds, walnuts, pistachios, and pecans, chopped

1 cup dates, chopped

2 cups apple juice

1 ripe banana, mashed

1/2 teaspoon cayenne pepper

1 teaspoon cinnamon, ground

1 tablespoon honey

Preheat oven to 370°.

Oil a round cake pan or a loaf pan.

Combine 4 eggs and 2 cups of sugar in a medium-size bowl. Blend with an electric mixer for about 3 minutes. Add the oil, flour, ginger, and nuts. Blend again, then add the dates, mashed banana, cayenne pepper, and cinnamon while adding the apple juice a little bit at a time. Don't add all the juice at one time so you can watch the mixture and make sure it isn't getting too runny. If it's getting too thick, add more juice. Blend with a wooden spoon or electric mixer for 3 to 4 minutes.

Pour the batter into the baking pan. Sprinkle some crushed nuts and drizzle honey on top. Shake the pan or tap it on the counter gently a few times to release the air bubbles. Bake for 40 to 50 minutes. Cool for 15 to 20 minutes before serving with tea or coffee.

Spicy Nut Cake

About the Author

Shahla Niazi

As a young child, Shahla knew the people of her small town believed in her grandmother Malec's healing skills and her uncanny knowledge of herbs and foods. A revered naturopath, herbalist, and healer, Malec taught Shahla about the unique properties of foods—hot versus cold—and how they work together to cure such ailments as an upset stomach. "See, Shahla," she would say, "this spice (ginger for example) paired with steamed Saffron rice will help to relieve the problem." The treasured book of Malec's notes on healing with foods and herbs was lost, but Shahla never forgot them.

Today Shahla continues the work her grandmother began with sacred recipes, gently handed down in memory and practice. She has documented and prepared hundreds of wonderful meals, each lovingly created with a purpose in mind: balancing the hot and cold properties of specific foods to provide the utmost in nutrition.

Shahla attended college in Australia, graduating with honors in photography and graphic design. She continues her research in the Dallas metropolitan area where she lives with her family.